# Misunderstood
# Texts of the
# New Testament

# Misunderstood Texts of the New Testament

Sir Robert Anderson

Biographical Sketch by
Warren W. Wiersbe

**KREGEL PUBLICATIONS**
Grand Rapids, Michigan 49501

*Misunderstood Texts of the New Testament*, by Sir
Robert Anderson. © 1991 by Kregel Publications, a
division of Kregel, Inc., P. O. Box 2607, Grand Rapids,
MI 49501. All rights reserved.

**Library of Congress Cataloging-in-Publication Data**

Anderson, Robert, Sir, 1841-1918.
    Misunderstood texts of the New Testament / Robert
Anderson.
        p.    cm.
    Reprint. Originally published: 1916.

    1. Bible. N.T.—Criticism, interpretation, etc.  I. Title.

BS2360.A53        1991        225.6—dc20    90-20618
                                            CIP
    ISBN    0-8254-2135-7  (paperback)

            2  3  4  5  Printing/Year  95  94  93

*Printed in the United States of America*

# Contents

# Scripture Index

# Biographical Sketch

Sir Robert Anderson described himself as "an anglicized Irishman of Scottish extraction." Before his death in 1918, he was widely recognized as a popular lay-preacher, an author of best-selling books on biblical subjects, and one of the most capable "defenders of the faith" at a time when "higher criticism" was threatening the church.

Robert Anderson was born in 1841 in Dublin, where his father, Matthew Anderson, served as Crown Solicitor for the city. His father was also a distinguished elder in the Irish Presbyterian Church. Robert was educated privately in Dublin, Paris, and Boulogne; and in 1859 he entered Trinity College, Dublin, graduating in 1862.

Brought up in a devout Christian home, Anderson in his late teens had serious doubts about his own conversion. About that time (1859-60) the Irish Revival was touching and changing the lives of many, including Robert's sister. She persuaded her brother to attend one of the services, but the popular hymns disturbed him and he got very little out of the the message. The following Sunday, he attended church and heard Dr. John Hall preach at the evening service. The message so disturbed him that he remained afterward to argue with the preacher.

In telling of the experience, Anderson wrote: ". . . facing me as we stood upon the pavement, he repeated with great solemnity his message and appeal: 'I tell you as a minister of Christ and in His name that there is life for you here and now, if you

will accept Him. Will you accept Christ or will you reject Him?'
. . . And I turned homeward with the peace of God filling my
heart."

Two years later, Anderson was active as a lay-preacher and
was greatly used to win many to Christ. In 1863 he was made a
member of the Irish Bar and served on the legal circuit. About
this time, the Fenians (a secret society attempting to overthrow
British Rule in Ireland) were at work, and he became involved
interrogating prisoners and preparing legal briefs. This was his
introduction into police work.

He was married in 1873 and four years later moved to London as a member of the Home Office staff. He had access to the
detective department and made good use of it. In 1888, while
Jack the Ripper was terrorizing London, Anderson moved into
Scotland Yard as Assistant Commissioner of Metropolitan Police and Chief of the Criminal Investigation Department. He
served his country well until his retirement in 1901, and the
records show that crime decreased in London during that period. Conan Doyle was entertaining London at that time with his
Sherlock Holmes stories, but it was Anderson and his staff who
were ridding the city of crime and criminals.

Anderson had a large circle of friends, not only politicians
but especially preachers: Dr. Handley G. Moule, J. Stuart Hold-
en, Henry Drummond, James M. Gray, C. I. Scofield, A. C. Dix-
on, and E. W. Bullinger, whose views on Israel and the church
greatly influenced Anderson. It was Horatius Bonar who first
taught Anderson the great truths concerning the second coming of Christ, and the "blessed hope" was a precious doctrine
to him, especially during the dark days of the first war.

He authored seventeen major books on biblical themes, and
it is good to see them coming back into print. Charles H. Spur-
geon said that Anderson's book *Human Destiny* was "the most
valuable contribution on the subject" that he had ever seen. His
last book, *Unfulfilled Prophecy and the Hope of the Church*, was
published in 1917. On November 15, 1918, Sir Robert Anderson
was called Home.

The books of Sir Robert Anderson underscore the inspiration and dependable authority of the Bible, the deity of Jesus
Christ, and the necessity of new birth. He tracked down myths

and religious error, arrested and exposed it, with the same skill and courage that he displayed when he tracked down criminals. If you have never met Sir Robert Anderson, then you are about to embark on a thrilling voyage of discovery. If he is already one of your friends, then finding a new Anderson title, or meeting an old one, will bring joy to your heart and enlightenment to your mind. Happy reading!

WARREN W. WIERSBE

# *Preface*

These pages were originally designed to be merely a series of expository notes upon certain passages of the New Testament. But this method of dealing with the texts selected from the first gospel proved inconvenient and unsatisfactory, for it involved a good deal of repetition in unconnected discourse respecting the scope and character of "Matthew." The scheme of an introductory chapter thus suggested itself. And the importance of this was emphasized by a "love your enemies" sermon preached just then in a prominent metropolitan pulpit— a sermon to which the secular newspapers accorded an extraordinary measure of publicity.

As maintained in these pages,[1] he must be but a poor type of Christian who can regard without feelings of aversion, deliberate and deep, either the evil men who are directly responsible for the fiendish crimes committed by our enemies in this war,[2] or the mass of the German people who not only condone but sympathize with them. This, however, is merely incidental, for the main question here dealt with is a flagrant misuse of the Sermon on the Mount, which has discredited the sacred words in the estimation of multitudes, no authoritative voice having been raised to correct the error.

Some there are who, though sharing the views here expressed,

---

1. See, *ex. gr.*, pp. 21, 22.
2. The author refers to World War I during which this book was written (Editor's note).

will resent the statement of them by a layman. But if, when no other voice was available, "a dumb ass" was divinely used to rebuke a prophet, surely, *faute de mieux*, "a mere layman" may rebuke a preacher. When in a like case Dante was charged with the sin of Uzzah, he pleaded that it was not upon the ark he had laid his hand, but only on the oxen that were endangering its safety.

The author has purposely limited his references to a few well-known authorities of high repute. And where he has referred to his own writings, he has done so merely for the sake of his very numerous readers in homes scattered throughout far off lands, where his other books have already found a welcome.

SIR ROBERT ANDERSON

Easter, 1916

# 1

# *Introduction*

"I tell you earnestly and authoritatively (I know I am right in this), you must get into the habit of looking intensely at words, assuring yourself of their meaning, syllable by syllable—nay, letter by letter."

These words of Ruskin's glaringly exaggerate the worth of mere human writings, but they might fitly be inscribed on the flyleaf of every Testament and Bible. For the words of God are like the works of God, in that we often need the microscope to enable us to appreciate them. And yet at times this element is of secondary importance. For, unless we understand the divine scheme and purpose of the Bible as a whole, we cannot read even the New Testament intelligently.

The following travesty of the teaching of Scripture is a fair statement of the views—beliefs we can scarcely call them— which are commonly held:

Adam's sin so thoroughly depraved the nature of his descendants, that God destroyed them in the Flood, and began again with Noah. But the Noachian dispensation was as great a failure as that which it succeeded. In the Babylonian apostasy, indeed, the corruption of the primeval revelation was so radical and permeating that even "the Christian religion" is leavened with its distinctive errors. So God then resorted to another plan. He singled out Abraham and his race to be His "peculiar people," and "unto them were committed the oracles of God." But if previous dispensations collapsed in failure, the Abrahamic

13

ended in disaster. For the covenant people crucified the Messiah when He came to fulfill to them the prophecies and promises of all the Scriptures. Therefore the divine purposes for earth, so plainly unfolded in those Scriptures, have now been jettisoned; and in this Christian dispensation—"the last great period of God's dealings with mankind"—earth is a mere recruiting-ground for heaven, and it will be given up to judgment fire as soon as the number of the elect has been completed.

Is it any wonder that the Bible is neglected by the profane, and that so much of it is accepted by the devout on the principle of "shut your eyes and open your mouth"? For this sort of biblical interpretation leaves the Old Testament an easy prey to the German "culture" of the infidel Higher Criticism crusade. And even in the case of the New Testament, not only isolated texts but considerable portions must needs be explained in the sense of being explained away.

Very specially does this apply to its opening and closing books. The loss of either of them would destroy the unity and completeness of the Bible. And yet the Book of Revelation is regarded as a mere appendix, provided for the entertainment of people of leisure with a taste for mysticism. And the first gospel is too often used to modify, if not to "correct," the teaching of the epistles. But the closing of the Canon might fitly be described as the stocktaking book of the Bible; for the unfulfilled prophecies and promises of the Hebrew Scriptures are there traced to their consummation. And Matthew supplies the link which binds the Old Testament to the New.

For the purpose of these pages, however, it will suffice to explain the place which the gospel of Matthew holds in the divine scheme of revelation. Our theology is largely based on the teaching of the Latin Fathers, and with them it was an accepted fact that God "cast away His people whom He foreknew." The prophecies relating to Israel, and to God's purposes of blessing for earth, have therefore to be spiritualized to make them applicable to the church. But the simple prose of Matthew will not allow of treatment of this kind. And so that gospel is regarded as a sort of poor relation of the others; whereas to the student of prophecy it is in some respects the most important book of the New Testament.

## A Portrait Gallery

The Gospels are not, as infidels suppose, imperfect and often conflicting records of the life and ministry of "Jesus," but separate portraits, as it were, of the Lord Jesus Christ with reference to His various relationships and offices. This appears very strikingly when we compare the first gospel with the fourth. For the fourth is the revelation of the Son of God, who came not to judge, but to save the world (John 12:7); whereas Matthew records His advent and ministry as Israel's Messiah; and we scan it in vain for words of the kind we value in the fourth gospel—words which we, as Gentiles, can take to ourselves without reserve.

This notable fact is not to be explained by suggesting that the apostle Matthew was a narrow-minded Jew who refused to identify himself with the teaching of his Lord whenever it passed beyond the sphere of Jewish hopes and interests. And the only alternative to this is that, writing by divine inspiration, he was so guided and restrained that nothing came from his pen, save what was strictly germane to the special revelation entrusted to him by the Holy Spirit.

"He was in the world, and the world was made by Him, and the world knew Him not (John 1:10)." Thus it is that the fourth gospel opens; while the first begins by recording His birth and lineage—not, indeed, as infidels would tell us, as the descendant of an Arab sheikh and petty tribal king, but as the promised "Seed" of Abraham, and as "David's greater Son"—the glories of whose coming reign over this earth of ours fill so prominent place in Hebrew Scripture.

To that reign it was that the Baptist's testimony pointed, when he came "preaching in the wilderness of Judea, and saying, Repent ye; for the kingdom of heaven is at hand (Matt. 3:1, 2)." The same testimony was afterwards taken up by the Lord Himself, and in due course entrusted to His apostles.[1] The popular belief that it was meant to herald what we call the "Christian dispensation" is utterly mistaken.

"The kingdom of the heavens" (for such is the right rendering of the Greek words) occurs thirty-three times in Matthew, and

---

1. John 3:1, 2; 4:17; 10:5, 9.

nowhere else in the New Testament. But what are we to understand by the phrase? It cannot mean that God would soon begin to rule the heavens! And the only possible alternative is that the time was near when He would assume the government of earth.

Much that is true of our island-home may be predicated of every land on which floats the "Union Jack" but England is not the British Empire. And there is a like distinction between the kingdom of heaven and the kingdom of God. They are not synonymous; for the kingdom of heaven relates exclusively to earth.

But here a strange fact claims notice. By untold millions of lips the prayer is daily uttered: "Thy kingdom come." And yet, with the unbeliever who uses that prayer, the suggestion of divine government on earth would be scorned as a dream of visionaries; and among believers there is not one in a hundred who would not be shocked at the suggestion that the kingdom has not already come. Does not Scripture tell us (they would indignantly exclaim) that "the Lord God omnipotent reigneth"?[2]

And it was not the crucifixion that postponed the fulfillment of the Lord's words. For His prayer upon the cross secured forgiveness for His murderers—witness the amnesty proclaimed at Pentecost by His inspired apostle (Acts 3:19-24). But the preaching of that Pentecostal gospel, first in Jerusalem, and afterwards throughout all Jewry and as far away as Rome, evoked never a response from even a local synagogue. The Acts of the Apostles contains the record of it and it closes with the "Ichabod" pronounced upon that unrepentant and guilty people. Instead, therefore, of sending "the Christ foreordained unto them," God sent the awful judgment that so soon engulfed them; and the times of the Gentiles, which had seemed about to end, have lingered on for nineteen centuries.

Though the purposes of God cannot be thwarted by the sins of men, the fulfillment of them may be thus postponed. And just as the wilderness apostasy of Israel prolonged their wanderings for forty years, although Canaan was but a few days march from Sinai, so the more gross apostasy of Christendom

---

2. See note on Revelation 19:6, *post.*

has prolonged for nigh two thousand years an era which the Lord and His apostles taught the early saints to look upon as brief.

Not that "the times of the Gentiles" are adjacent with "the Christian dispensation." The subjection of the Jewish nation to the supremacy of Babylon was the epoch of that era; and it will continue until the restoration of their national polity—an event which awaits the return of their Messiah. According to words familiar to every Jew, "His feet shall stand in that day upon the Mount of Olives, which is before Jerusalem on the east" (Zech. 14:4). And when upon the day of the Ascension the disciples saw Him standing there, forgetful of the warning He had given them so recently,[3] they put to Him the question: "Wilt Thou at this time restore the kingdom to Israel?" And the Lord's reply implicitly accredited the question as Scriptural and right, albeit it was not for them to know "times or seasons" (Acts 1:8, 7). Here, then, is a principle to guide us in studying the Scriptures. Divine promises and prophecies are not like bank checks that become invalid by lapse of time. Every word "which God hath spoken by the mouth of all His holy prophets since the world began" about "the times of restitution of all things" (Acts 3:21)— that is, the times when all things shall be put right on earth— shall be fulfilled as literally as were the seemingly incredible predictions of Bethlehem and Calvary. And when the Lord proclaimed that the kingdom of heaven was at hand, He meant that the time was near when these "times of restitution" would bring peace and blessedness to this sin-blighted world.

## Messianic Prophecies

Let us then apply this to His teaching at the close of His ministry, as recorded in the gospel of Matthew. No one could have imagined that between the fulfillment of the great prophecy of Isaiah 53 and of the prophecy which immediately follows it, there would be an interval of twenty centuries; or that a like period would intervene between the fulfillment of the prophe-

---

3. When upon that same Mount of Olives, the disciples asked Him, "What shall be the sign of Thy coming, and of the consummation of the age?" (Matthew 24:3, Revised Version.). "The end of the world" is a faulty translation; the age they were thinking of was, of course, the time of the Gentiles.

cy of Matthew 24 and the event which the Lord foretold in the
second verse of that same chapter. But the explanation of this
will plainly appear if we bear in mind, first, that all Messianic
prophecy relating to earth runs in the channel of Israel's national history; and therefore, so to speak, the clock of prophetic
time is stopped while their national history is in abeyance. And
secondly, that Israel's rejection during this Christian dispensation is a New Testament "mystery."[4]

It was not that our Lord spoke in ignorance. But though His
divine knowledge was full and absolute, His use of that knowledge, during all His earthly ministry, was subject to definite
limitations. For He never spoke save as the Father gave Him to
speak, and "times and seasons" the Father had kept in His own
*exousia* (Acts 1:7).

As we read these Scriptures, we must bear in mind that the
kingdom of heaven is for earth, and that the earthly people of
the Abrahamic promise are the divinely appointed agency for
the administration of it. And Matthew is the gospel that speaks
of it, because it is the gospel which reveals Christ in His relationships with the earthly people. And if we are to understand
that gospel aright, we need to give a first reading to much of it
as from the standpoint of the disciples to whom it was specially
addressed. For the man of God "all Scripture is profitable," and
therefore none may be neglected. But we must distinguish between interpretation and application. And, above all, we must
clear our minds from the ignorance of Latin theology. "God
hath *not* cast away His people whom He foreknew"; and in His
own good time "all Israel shall be saved." Not, as the apostle
explains, that every Israelite shall be saved, but that Israel as a
nation shall be restored to the place assigned to them in Holy
Scripture (Romans 11:2, 25-29).

The scheme of the first gospel is as definite as it is simple. It
opens, as we have seen, by recording the birth of Christ as the
"Seed" of the Abrahamic covenant, and the King of Israel. Then

---

4. Romans 11:25. In the New Testament use a mystery signifies "not a thing
unintelligible, but what lies hidden and secret till made known by the revelation of
God." These are Bloomfield's words. Dr. Sandy, of Oxford, defines it as "something
which up to the time of the apostles had remained secret, but had been made known
by divine intervention."

we have John the Baptist's ministry, which was a *provisional* fulfillment of the promised advent of Elijah (see Matthew 11:14). Then, after the Temptation, the Lord Himself proclaimed the same gospel of the coming kingdom, and accredited His testimony by that marvellous display of miraculous power recorded at the close of chapter 4. In the three succeeding chapters He unfolded to His disciples the principles of the kingdom. In chapter 10 He commissioned the Twelve to take up the kingdom ministry; and the following chapter chronicles a series of typical acts and utterances of power, and mercy, and judgment. In chapter 12 we reach a crisis in the ministry.

Just as by "spiritualizing" all the prophecies relating to His earthly kingdom glories, the "Christian church" has either perverted or ignored them, so by a like process the "Jewish church" perverted or ignored the prophecies relating to His earthly sufferings and death. And therefore the abundant proofs of His Messiahship had no voice for men who were looking only for the Son of David to deliver them from the Roman yoke; and the Sanhedrin decided that "the Galilean" was an impostor, and they decreed His death (Matt. 12:14).

His ministry forthwith entered upon a new phase. Till then, His teaching had been open and plain; but now it became veiled in parables (ch. 13). As those evil men had scorned His testimony, they were now to heal without understanding, and to see without perceiving (v. 14). None but His disciples were to know the *mysteries* of the kingdom of heaven—mysteries, namely, a phase of things till then unrevealed.[5] The Hebrew Scriptures spoke of a king coming to reign, the Lord now speaks of a sower going forth to sow. This was not merely an enigma to the Jewish leaders, it must have deepened their hostility; and the meaning of it was explained to none but His own disciples (v. 11).

An analysis of the succeeding chapters would point the same moral and be no less important; for across every section of the book may be inscribed the words, "He came unto His own, and His own received Him not (John 1:11)." But for our present purpose a further notice of "the second Sermon on the Mount" will suffice; and even this will involve some repetition.

---

5. See footnote, p. 7, *ante.*

To understand the Lord's teaching in these twenty-fourth and twenty-fifth chapters, I repeat with emphasis, we must give them a first reading from the standpoint of those to whom they were addressed—Hebrew disciples, who were rightly looking for the restoration of the kingdom to Israel. Messiah had come, and was in their midst. But, in some way that is not told us, they had learned that there was to be yet another "coming," to wind up the age of Gentile supremacy, and to bring in "the times of restitution of all things." And these chapters record the Lord's reply to their inquiry, "What shall be the sign of Thy coming and of the winding-up of the age?" (Not its *telos*, but its *sunteleia*.)

## The Two Comings

It seems extraordinary that any student of Scripture should fail to distinguish between the coming of the Lord to call His people away to heaven at the close of this Christian dispensation, and His coming as Son of Man to establish His kingdom upon earth. But the writings of the Fathers have such a dominating influence upon the theology of Christendom that this confusion is enshrined as truth. The various Scriptures which tell of the future appearing of Christ have all been "thrown into hotchpot" (as the lawyers would say), and the doctrine of "the Second Advent" is the result.

These Scriptures have nothing in common, save that they speak of the same Christ. I will not deal here with the last great coming at the end of all things.[6] But the language of the Epistles respecting that coming which Bengel calls "the hope of the church,"[7] gives color to the figment that it will be entirely secret: whereas Scripture is explicit that His coming as the Son of Man to earth will be open and manifest. And in foretelling it, the Lord emphatically warned the disciples that it would not take place until after certain notable events and movements foretold in Hebrew prophecy; whereas, in marked contrast with

6. I do not mean to imply that there will be only three future "comings" of Christ. But the distinction between the three here noted is as clear and certain in Scripture as language can make it. And this suffices for our present purpose.

7. John Bengel, *Bengel's New Testament Commentary* (Grand Rapids: Kregel Publications, 1981), vol. 2.

this, the early saints of this dispensation were taught by the inspired apostles to live in constant expectation of His coming. And there is not a word in the epistles to suggest that any event foretold in prophecy must intervene before the fulfillment of "that blessed hope." And the long delay in its fulfillment is amply accounted for by the hopeless and shameless apostasy of the professing church on earth, even from the earliest times.

The World War [I] now raging is not the fulfillment of Revelation 16:16. For "a place called in the Hebrew tongue Armageddon" is not situated in either France or Flanders, but in Palestine; and the future of the land and people of the covenant will be a main issue in the great battle yet to be fought on that historic plain. And yet the present war may result in preparing the stage for the resumption of the drama of Hebrew prophecy. For if the Turk should be expelled from the Holy Land, it seems reasonably certain that Palestine will become a protected Jewish State. A protected State, I say advisedly, for until the end of "the times of the Gentiles" the Jews are to remain subject to Gentile rulership.

The Lord's words in Matthew 24:15 refer explicitly to the seventieth week of Daniel (9:27). Some future "Kaiser" will make a treaty with the Jews, guaranteeing the free observance of their religion. And his violation of that treaty after three and a half years—"in the midst of the week"—will be the epoch of "the great tribulation," a persecution unparalleled in all the past (v. 21). And as the Lord tells us in verse 29, the tribulation will be followed "immediately" by the appalling convulsions in the sphere of nature which are to usher in the day of the Lord (Isaiah 13:9, 10; Joel 12:31).

This exposition of Matthew 24 is strikingly confirmed by the apocalyptic visions. For under the fifth seal we have the martyrs of the tribulation (Rev. 6:9); and the events of the sixth seal (v. 12) are identical with those which the Lord declared would immediately follow the tribulation (Matt. 24:29).

So far all is clear. But owing to the ambiguity of a minor word in the thirtieth verse, the sequel is commonly misread. The Greek *tote* has a meaning as elastic as our English "then." And here, as in the first verse of chapter 25, it covers the whole period between the end of the tribulation and the coming of the

Son of Man. And the signal change in the Lord's teaching at this point claims very special notice. He had warned the disciples to watch, *not for His coming*, but for the events which must precede it. But now, the tribulation past, these events are all fulfilled, and His word is, "Watch, for ye know not what hour your Lord doth come"(v. 42).

The duration of that waiting period we cannot estimate, save that apparently it will be within the lifetime of that generation (v. 34). But it will be sufficiently prolonged to make the world forget the preceding terrors (vv. 38, 39), and to make His people need repeated exhortations to continued watchfulness. For though signs and portents mark the *santeleia* of that future age, the coming of the Son of Man will be unheralded and sudden (v. 44).

This is the event foretold by the Lord in Matthew 24:30, 31, and again in 25:31; and the intervening passage contains His teaching relating to the waiting period between the end of the tribulation and His actual coming. For here, as so often in the prophetic Scriptures, after the ultimate issue is declared, a prophecy is interposed leading up to the same goal. The Lord's second and fuller statement of it is as follows:

"When the Son of Man shall come in His glory, and all the holy angels with Him, then shall He sit on the throne of His glory, and before Him shall be gathered all nations . . ." (Matt. 25: 31, 32).

This is indeed a "misunderstood text"! For under the influence of patristic theology, eminent commentators would have us believe that it describes "the great and universal judgment, in which all the dead, small and great, shall stand before God. Revelation 20:11-15." The editor of the *Speaker's Commentary* declares that "it is hardly possible" to regard it in any other light. But Revelation 20 and Matthew 25 have absolutely nothing in common save that both relate to sessions of divine judgment. The one is a judgment of the dead, in a vastly remote future; the other is a judgment of living nations upon earth, and, for aught we know, it may fall within the lifetime of the present generation. For the Lord's words imply that, but for the intervention of the present "mystery" dispensation, the disciples to whom they were addressed might have witnessed their fulfillment. And, as already suggested, the hands of the clock of prophetic time will again begin to move after His coming to bring this dispensation to an end.

We have no definite data by which to measure either the interval between that coming and the beginning of the seventieth week of Daniel, or the interval between the end of that week and His coming as Son of Man. We know, however, that before His coming to His earthly people "the gospel of the kingdom will be preached in the whole world for a testimony to all the nations " (Matt. 24.14) —not the gospel of this age of grace, but the *gospel of the kingdom.* And the last fourteen verses of chapter 25 are explicit, that the question at issue in the judgment will be the treatment of the messengers accredited to proclaim that gospel to the world. This is no novel principle. As the Lord had already said to His disciples, "He that receiveth you receiveth Me." And wherever the gospel comes, it is receiving or rejecting Christ that fixes the destiny of men.

But it may be asked, How could hundreds of millions of people appear before the Son of Man on earth? Just in the same way that, in the ages succeeding this very judgment, they will go up to Jerusalem year by year to keep the Feast of Tabernacles (Zech. 14:16). Their accredited leaders will represent them.[8] To read Scripture aright we need both spiritual intelligence and common sense. If the spiritual fitness be lacking, we shall refuse to believe anything that seems to go beyond our ordinary experience; and a want of common sense will often betray us into an excessive literalness that may make the language of Scripture seem impossible.

But is not this narrative so incredible that we are reasonably justified in refusing to take it literally? If that is to be the test, we may at once reject the great truths of revelation—the Incarnation, the Atonement, the Resurrection, the Ascension. For in the wildest superstitions of false religions there is nothing so incredible as these truths. But our spiritual being is by nature so depraved that we are ready to believe anything, whether it be a seemingly transparent lie, like transubstantiation, or a

---

8. Thus it was that the myriads of Israel in the wilderness were sprinkled with the blood of the covenant (Ex. 24:8). And many other illustrations of the principle might be cited.

seemingly impossible truth, like "the Virgin Birth," provided it is conditioned in our religion! But there we draw the line. And the great "mystery" truths of this Christian dispensation, including the coming of the Lord, as revealed in the Epistles, and also the truths of the kingdom, including the coming of the Son of Man, as foretold by the Lord Himself, have not been thus accustomed; and so they are either rejected or ignored.

True it is, no doubt, as already noticed, that Christendom, million-mouthed, uses the divinely given words, "Thy kingdom come; Thy will be done on earth as it is done in heaven." But with the mass of men this is merely a meaningless incantation. For such is "the covert atheism" of our nature, that though we are willing to believe in a "Second Advent," provided it be too remote to affect us in any way, we are slow to believe in a "coming" that is a present hope, to influence our daily life. And just in the same way we are willing to believe in a kingdom of heaven beyond the stars. But when the infidel intelligently argues that, if our God were not a myth, He would establish His rule upon this earth of ours; instead of making the reply which ought to be ready on our lips, we throw into "hotchpot" all that Scripture teaches about the kingdom of God, and the church of God, and the kingdom of heaven; and over the incongruous mass we indulge in feeble platitudes about divine wisdom and goodness!

And in an age of keen, intelligent activity, this method of "handling the Word of God" has done more than aggressive infidelity to undermine faith. It has driven multitudes to skepticism. To its baneful influence is due the success of the infidel crusade which masquerades as "Higher Criticism"—a movement that has degraded Germany to its present level of barbarism, and has so corrupted "organized Christianity" in Britain that there is not one of the churches of the Reformation that would hold together if called upon to give corporately an unequivocal and explicit testimony, such as in other days they gave with united voice, to the deity of Christ and the divine origin, truth, and authority of the Bible as the Word of God.

Though the follies and falsehoods of this movement have been thoroughly exposed and refuted, it has taught men to shake free from traditional beliefs, and to study these subjects with an open mind. And it is because our divinity schools and theological seminaries teach the theology of the Fathers, instead of teaching the Bible, that so many of their alumni are either the dupes of medieval superstition or the exponents of a half faith which is near allied to skepticism.

## The Truth Was Lost

Plain words are needed here. In the interval between the apostolic age and the era of the patristic theologians, the main truths of the distinctively Christian revelation were lost in the early church; and they were never fully recovered until the evangelical revival of the nineteenth century. But our commentators ignore the revival, and continue to trade upon the writings of the Fathers. And the results are disastrous. For while an intelligent study of Scripture always tends to faith, the Christianized infidelity which now prevails in our churches is largely due to a revolt against the traditional exegesis of Scripture. And so, as Adolph Saphir wrote, "It is out of the arsenal of the orthodox that the very fundamental truths of the Gospel have been assailed." For, he added, this traditional interpretation "paved the way for Rationalism and Neology."

If *Christians* fail to distinguish between what the Scriptures teach, and what men teach about the Scriptures, it is not strange that unbelievers should be thus misled. And so it comes about that the orthodox of one generation sow seeds of skepticism for the next. Some of us remember, for example, when it was taught as "Bible truth" that the reign of righteousness and peace on earth would come automatically by the preaching of the gospel. But people who had a better knowledge, both of the Bible and of human nature, gave no heed to a delusion so baseless and so foolish. Nor did we need the horrors and infamies of German *Kultur* to teach us that earth can never be the home of peace and happiness, save under the stern and righteous government of Heaven.

And in the same way a misuse of Matthew 24 is now sowing seeds of skepticism to be reaped in the near future. For it is asked, Is not this World War [ I ] the fulfillment of the Lord's words recorded in that chapter? Some are thus led to infer that a supreme crisis in earth's history is so near that efforts for the extension of missionary enterprise may be relaxed. And others again are clear that the war will be followed by an era of millennial peace. And the champions of these rival errors appeal to Scripture with equal confidence. But while the second Sermon on the Mount may throw much light on events and movements of our own day, both on the battlefield and in the professing church, the fulfillment of that great prophecy belongs to a future age. And Christians who, ignoring this, declare *ex cathedra* that they indeed have acquired a knowledge of "times and seasons," denied to the apostles of the Lord, are recklessly sowing evil seed which may hereafter choke the faith crop of many fields.

Scripture warns us that "in the last days perilous times shall come"; and proofs are many that those times may be close upon us. But we seem to be blind to their significance and their perils. In wartime the decks of our battleships are ruthlessly cleared of everything that might imperil safety. And though "the children of this world are wiser than the children of light (Luke 16:8)," they are not wiser than divine Scripture; as witness the apostle's words in view of the incipient apostasy of the early church, "I commend you to God and the word of His grace." But in these days, when the apostasy has developed with a force and subtlety unknown in all the past, instead of taking heed to the warning and the exhortation, and falling back on Holy Scripture, we refuse to jettison the "top hamper" of traditional exegesis. And as the result of this, and of thus ignoring the great "mystery" truths revealed in the Epistles, the whole scheme of the biblical revelation is dislocated, all sense of its divine unity is lost, and faith in its divine authority is undermined.

Those of us who have watched the course of the German infidel movement ever since it gained a foothold in Britain, must recognize that it is energized by a sinister spiritual influence which makes it indifferent to controversy. But to some of us that movement has proved "a blessing in disguise," for it has taught us to study the Bible with a mind untrammeled by the exegesis of early church fathers. And as the result we have attained a more intelligent, and therefore a firmer, faith in Holy Scripture as the Word of God.

## A Personal Experience

A personal experience is sometimes helpful to others. When I became a Christian in the truer sense of the word, I supposed that skeptical difficulties respecting the Gospels would no longer trouble me. But I was distressed to find that the more closely I studied them, the attempt to harmonize them seemed to become more hopeless. While in this state of mind I heard a lecture which ran somewhat on the lines indicated in the preceding pages. The effect of it was electric. It was a revelation to me; and I began to study the Gospel of Matthew with fresh intelligence and new interest. Every section of it seemed to glow with new light, a light that threw its rays back upon the Hebrew Scriptures, and forward to the Apocalypse. And I came to realize, as I had never realized before, the "hidden harmony " of the Bible as a whole.

The headmaster of Eton's "Love your enemies" sermon, preached in St. Margaret's, Westminster, on March 25, 1915, gave striking proof how a misreading of the first gospel may bring Holy Scripture into contempt. His purpose was to urge that the conduct of the war with Germany should be governed by the precepts of the Sermon on the Mount. If such a proposition had emanated from a secular publicist, it might have passed without notice. But it was put forward, ex cathedra, as the teaching of Scripture, by an officially accredited exponent of Scripture. And as the result, it was assumed by the secular press, and by men of the world generally, that this folly had scriptural sanction.

"Love your enemies" is the last in a group of precepts which the Lord enjoined upon His disciples in view of their mission as ministers of grace. They were not to resist evil. If struck upon one cheek they were to turn the other cheek. If a thief took their coat they were to let him take their cloak also. They were to give to every applicant, and to turn away from no would-be borrower (Matt. 10:39-44).

Could a country be governed on the lines of these precepts? or a public school? Why, if even a shopkeeper in a village street were to conduct his business in this way, he would be bankrupt within a month! And yet these were the words of the Lord of Glory; and, like all His words, they are divine and eternal. But He prefaced them by the warning that they were not to be taken as destroying "the law and the prophets"—a phrase which every Hebrew would rightly understand to mean what we Christians call the Old Testament Scriptures. And with still greater definiteness He declared that not "one jot or one tittle" of the law was abrogated by His teaching (vv. 17, 18). And yet both in his sermon and in his letters to the press in defense of it, Dr. Lyttelton assumed that the teaching of the Sermon on the Mount has entirely superseded the Old Testament Scriptures; whereas it is mainly by these very Scriptures that we ought to be guided in our conduct of affairs in every sphere of public life.

But in fulfilling their ministry of grace, His disciples were not to appeal to law. While He was with them they were to act as He acted. And at the close of their mission He asked them, in view of His leaving them, "When I sent you without purse, and scrip, and shoes, lacked ye anything?" "But now [He went on to say] he that hath a purse let him take it, and likewise his scrip; and he that hath no sword, let him sell his garment and buy one" (Luke 22:35, 36). In other words, they were to fall back on their position as citizens. Peter, Oriental though he was, took these last words literally; but we understand them better. Living in a civilized community, we carry the sword by proxy. If any one strikes us on the cheek, or steals our coat, we hand him over to the police; and the magistrate awards a fitting punishment, to which the jailer takes charge. But if, instead of seizing and punishing the law-breaker, these officers of the law treated him in accordance with the precepts of the Sermon on the Mount, they would "bear the sword in vain," and utterly fail in their duty as "the ministers of God" (Rom. 13:4).

But the police and the criminal courts can deal only with crimes committed within the realm. In the case of crimes committed by an alien enemy, recourse must be had to the naval and military forces of the Crown. But here the same principle applies. And with a far greater definiteness; for in the case of crimes committed by a nation, there is no room for sentiment or pity, which might claim a hearing in the case of individual offenders.

My purpose here is to expose and refute a flagrant misuse of the Sermon on the Mount. And let no one suppose that this involves our ignoring its application to ourselves. Though, in common with not a little of the Lord's teaching recorded in the first gospel, its full and final purpose will not be realized until the future age of the kingdom, its words of grace ought to have a special voice for His people in this dispensation of grace. If, for example, some Christian who is mourning the death of a dearly loved relative or friend, wantonly butchered in cold blood in this ghastly war, could come face to face with the German murderer, grace would teach him to show his love for his enemy by telling him of gospel pardon even for a crime so heinous and so hateful.

But this has nothing in common with that ill advised sermon. A notable commentary upon it was supplied by sermons preached last Christmas in Berlin and other German towns. Here are typical extracts from published reports of them:

Pastor Zoebel, speaking in the great Lutheran Church in Leipzig, referred to the German guns beating down the children of Satan, and to German submarines as "instruments to execute the divine vengeance," to send to the bottom of the sea thousands of the non-elect. "There ought to be no compromise with hell, no mercy for the servants of Satan— in other words, no pity for the English, French, and Russians; nor, indeed, for any nation that has sold itself to the devil. They have all been condemned to death by a divine decree."

Professor Rheinold Seeby, a teacher of theology in the Berlin University, preaching in the Cathedral of the city, said that in killing their enemies, burning their houses, and invading their territories, the Germans simply performed a work of charity.

Pastor Fritz Philippi, of Berlin, preaching from his Protestant pulpit on the divine mission of Germany, said that as the Almighty allowed His Son to be crucified that the scheme of redemption might be accomplished, so Germany was destined to crucify humanity, in order that its salvation might be secured. The human race could only be saved by blood, fire, and sword. "It is really because we are pure that we have been chosen by the Almighty as His instruments to punish the envious, to chastise the wicked, and to slay with the sword the sinful nations. The divine mission of Germany, oh brethren! is to crucify humanity; the duty of German soldiers, therefore, is to strike without mercy. They must kill, burn, and destroy, and any half measures would be wicked. Let it then be a war without pity."

He must be a poor sort of Christian who can regard such men, and their countless sympathizers of the pews, without feelings of aversion, deliberate and deep. Do we not well to remember the Lord's emphatic commendation of the church of Ephesus: "Thou canst not tolerate evil men"? (Rev. 2:2; cf. Matt. 18:17). It is not for us to anticipate the divine judgment respecting the eternal destiny of these men. What concerns us has regard to our attitude toward them here and now; and to recognize them as Christians would betoken disloyalty to Christ.

# 2

# Misunderstood Texts in the Gospels

*Which of you by taking thought can add one cubit to his stature?* (Matthew 6:27; Luke 12:25).

All the Lord's words were the expression of divine wisdom, but the words here attributed to Him savor of human folly. During "the great war" many a would-be recruit has longed to be an inch or two taller; but no one except "a freak dwarf " ever wished to add half a yard to his height! Moreover, no sane person could imagine that this might be attained by "taking thought"; and yet, according to our text, the Lord represented it as a mere trifle in comparison with the ordinary cares of life.

The primary and common meaning of *hêlikia* is age. But this growth in years brings physical development, the word acquired the secondary meaning of "stature"; and it is used in that sense in Luke 19:3. In Luke 2:52, also, it is thus translated. But Bloomfield there renders it *age*, "as being more agreeable to classic usage" (*Greek Testament*); and in his note on Ephesians 4:13, the same eminent Greek scholar writes, "*hêlikia* here does not mean *stature*, but *full age*"; that is, the maturity of our spiritual being—a correction that throws new light upon the passage. So, also, in John 9:21 and 23 the parents of the blind man to whom the Lord gave sight said, "He is of age, ask him." In Hebrews 9:11, the only other passage where the word occurs, it means "the time of life" in a special sense.

31

In the Revised Version, the phrase "taking thought" rightly gives place to "being anxious." The Christian should be always thoughtful, but never anxious; always careful, but never full of care. The Lord's words then might be freely rendered, "Who of you by giving way to anxiety can add a single step to the length of his life path?" Reasonable care may extend it by many a cubit, but corroding anxiety can only tend to shorten it. When writing his father's memoir, the late Sir James Paget, the eminent surgeon, used the striking phrase that his death was due to "that rarest of all causes of death, old age!" And it is not the aged only who undesignedly commit suicide through failing to "take thought."

> *Enter ye in at the strait gate. . . . Because strait is the gate, and narrow is the way, which leadeth unto life, and few there be that find it* (Matthew 7:13, 14).

We are told that in Eastern cities there are small gates in out-of-the-way corners, which are approached by "straitened" (R.V.) and little-used paths, which would be noticed only by those who seek for them.[1] And, of course, such gates and paths are in striking contrast to the great city gate and the main road which leads to it. The allegory of these verses would be understood by all to whom the Lord was speaking. But Westerners seem to miss its meaning.

As the "wide gate," to which the broad way leads, symbolizes destruction, the narrow gate must symbolize life. And therefore the usual exegesis, that the "straitened way" symbolizes a holy walk, is in direct opposition to the teaching of the passage and to the truth of the gospel. For there can be no holiness of walk until we receive life as God's gift in grace. Moreover, the warning which immediately follows, beginning with the words, "Beware of false prophets," plainly indicates that the contrast which the Lord intends is not between an evil life and a holy life, but between "religion" and *Himself*. No sane man believes that divine favor can be won by an evil life. But that it is to be

---

1. James Neil, *Everyday Life in the Holy Land* (p. 155). See note on Luke 13:24, *post*.

won by a *religious* life is the creed of the human heart the wide world over.

And this perverted instinct of human nature leads many real Christians to misread any passage of Scripture that can be perverted to indicate that the seeming simplicity and "trueness" of the gospel must be taken with reserve, and that its words are not to be trusted in the way we can trust the words of honorable men. For the sinner must needs *seek* for the way which leads to life, and *knock* at the door when he finds it; and this we are told is not so easy as the words would lead us to suppose! If any reader of this page should harbor such a thought, let him mark the words which preface the invitation of verse 13, "Every one that asketh receiveth; and he that seeketh findeth; and to him that knocketh it shall be opened" (v. 8).

*The Son of Man hath not where to lay His head* (Matthew 8:20).

This is the first occurrence of this Messianic title in the New Testament, and in Scripture a first occurrence is often significant. In the Old Testament—as, for example, in Ezekiel—"Son of Man" is often used as an emphatic Hebraism for *man*; but John 5:27 is the only New Testament passage where it occurs in this sense. Because He is *man*, all judgment is committed to the Lord Jesus. The English reader misses the significance which the Greek article lends to the words elsewhere; but it is recognized by scholars. And there can be no doubt as to the significance which the Lord Himself attached to this, His favorite title. When, for example, He here exclaimed, "The foxes have holes and the birds of the air have nests, but the Son of Man hath not where to lay His head," it is clear that the contrast His words were intended to enforce was between the highest and the lowest. The humblest creature has a home, but He, the Son of Man, "descended from heaven," was an outcast wanderer. And on the last occasion on which He used the title, when on His defense before the Sanhedrin, His purpose in declaring Himself to be the Son of Man of Daniel's vision (7:13) was to assert His personal and inherent right to heavenly glory.

For it was not His human birth that constituted Him the Son

of Man. That birth was indeed the fulfillment of the promise which the name implied; but, as He declared explicitly, the Son of Man "descended out of heaven" (John 3:13); and He added, "who is in heaven," which, as Alford notices, certainly implies "whose place is in heaven." And again He said, "What and if ye shall see the Son of Man ascend up where He was before?" (John 6:72). When, therefore, He proclaims that "the Son of Man came to seek and to save that which was lost"— "came to give His life a ransom for many"—faith responds in the language of that noble hymn, "When Thou tookest upon Thee to deliver man, Thou didst not abhor the virgin's womb." For the Virgin Birth was but a stage in the fulfillment of His mission. And this throws light upon the words of the creation story, "Let us make man in our image, after our likeness" (Gen. 1:26). For the "type"—using the word in the biologist's sense—is not the creature of Eden, but He after whose likeness the creature was fashioned.

One point more. Though the title "the Son of Man" occurs so frequently in relation to the earthly people of the covenant, the Lord is never so designated with reference to His heavenly people of this Christian age. Never once, therefore, is it found in the Epistles—a fact that exposes, and ought to bar, the error which is so generally accepted as truth, that "the coming of the Son of Man" of Matthew 24 and elsewhere in the first Gospel, is the same event as the Lord's coming to bring this "Christian dispensation" to an end, and to call His heavenly people home.

*Ye shall not have gone over the cities of Israel till the Son of Man be come* (Matthew 10:23).

This statement must apparently be dismissed as a hopeless enigma, or rejected as a sheer blunder. But to the Christian who has learned to recognize the dispensational and prophetic character of Matthew's Gospel, its meaning is clear; and a perusal of the preceding introductory chapter will render further explanation unnecessary.[2] "The hope of the church"—to use Ben-

---

2. See especially pages 12-14. The First Gospel is misunderstood if its prophetic character be ignored. Some commentators, for example, explain this verse by reference to the destruction of Jerusalem, as also ch. 15:28. (See pages 36, 37, *post.*)

gel's phrase—is not "the coming of the Son of Man" to earth in fulfillment of Messianic prophecy, but the coming of the Lord Jesus Christ to call up to heaven His people of the heavenly election of the present dispensation. And this dispensation, and the distinctive truths relating to it, were "mysteries" unrevealed until the earthly people were set aside. But these, and other similar words, will be received and acted on by Hebrew disciples in days to come, just as they would have been received and acted on by the disciples of the Lord's earthly ministry if the Christian dispensation had not intervened.

> *Verily I say unto you, Among them that are born of women there hath not risen a greater than John the Baptist: notwithstanding he that is least in the kingdom of heaven is greater than he* (Matthew 11:11).

As the Revised Version margin reminds us, the Greek is the comparative, not the superlative. But "he that is lesser" is intolerable as an English rendering. We might read it "the little one," a word that the Lord uses of His disciples in chapter 10:42. Although the great Chrysostom adopted it, the gloss that the Lord was thus referring to Himself is really unworthy of consideration. "For such an interpretation is surely adverse to the spirit of the whole discourse. We may certainly say that our Lord in such a passage as this would not designate Himself as *'he that is least'* compared with John, in any sense" (Alford). And it is certain that "the little one in the Kingdom" is not *personally* greater than the greatest of the prophets. It is clearly a question of *dispensational* position. The prophets were heralds of the coming kingdom; whereas, now, even the humblest disciple was a citizen of the kingdom.

And the same applies in principle to the heavenly election of the Body of Christ. The least of its members is greater than the greatest of a bygone economy; not personally—far from it—but *dispensationally.* Some of us who are inclined to think highly of ourselves, here and now, will appear very small indeed *personally* in comparison until the faith heroes whose names are enshrined in the honor roll of Hebrews 11.

*And from the days of John the Baptist, until now, the kingdom of heaven suffereth violence, and the violent take it by force* (Matthew 11:12).

This verse is a veritable crux; and expositors generally convey the impression that they are not satisfied with the explanations they give of it. The rendering of our English versions clearly suggests the thought of a hostile, aggressive movement against the kingdom of heaven. But this is quite foreign to the context. And surely the way in which the main word, on which the exegesis of the verse depends, was used by the Lord in a kindred passage ought to guide us here.

In Luke 16:16 we read, "The law and the prophets were until John: since that time the kingdom of God is preached, and every man presseth into it." Now, the word here rendered "presseth into it" is identical with that which is translated "suffereth violence" in our present verse (Matt. 11:12). And one of its lexicon meanings is, "to carry a point by obstinate perseverance." Can there be any doubt then that the Lord was here referring, not to a hostile movement against the kingdom, but to the forceful impetuosity of His nominal disciples? For example, the thousands of men whom He fed to satisfaction with a basketful of bread and fish were so eager to proclaim Him King that He had to hide Himself from them. And that this was His meaning here is established by the fact that the word rendered "take it by force," is that which occurs in John 6:15, "When Jesus perceived that they would come and take Him by force, to make Him a King, He departed again into a mountain Himself alone."

The attitude and conduct of the Jewish leaders toward Him were marked, not by violence, but by mingled hatred, cunning, and timidity. Again and again they would have seized Him, but that they feared the people. And if the Lord hid Himself from the provincial Jews, it was not because they were hostile, but because, knowing what was in man, He would not "commit Himself unto them," for they were merely miracle-made disciples (John 2:23-25). Or, to use the apostle's phrase in Galatians 2:15, they were merely "Jews by nature." Just as now, "all who profess and call themselves Christians" are nominally the people of God, so was it then with Jews. And every Jew was looking for the Messiah. But the "Jews by nature" wanted a Messiah who would free them from the Roman yoke. And they rightly judged that a man with seemingly unlimited miraculous powers could win their deliverance. Their hopes were carnal, and they were ready to attain the realization of them by carnal means. Thus it was that "the kingdom of heaven was suffering violence."

*So shall the Son of Man be three days and three nights in the heart of the earth* (Matthew 12:40).

Some people find here a clear proof that Scripture has erred; others that the Lord was crucified on Thursday. But in this both critics and "reconcilers" merely display their ignorance. "Three days and three nights" was a familiar idiomatic phrase to cover a period that included any part of three days. We need not go outside Scripture to exemplify this. The Egyptian mentioned in 1 Samuel 30:11-13 had had neither food nor drink for "three days and three nights," and yet it was only three days since he had fallen sick. So, again, in 2 Chronicles 10:5, 12, we read that Rehoboam said to the Israelites, "Come again unto me *after three days* . . . so they came to him *on the third day.*" And in Esther 4:16 and 5:1, we are told that the queen ordered a fast for three days, and yet she held a banquet on the third day.

But Matthew 27:63, 64 would settle the question, even if it stood alone. Twenty-four hours after the Lord's burial, the Jews came to Pilate and said, "We remember that that deceiver said, while he was yet alive, *After three days* I will rise again. Command, therefore, that the sepulcher be made sure *until the third day.*" And if that Sunday had passed, leaving the seal upon the tomb unbroken, the guard would have been withdrawn, and the Pharisees would have proclaimed their triumph. In nine passages do the Gospels record His words that He would rise "on the third day"; and in 1 Corinthians 15:4 the apostle Paul proclaimed the fact as an integral part of the gospel.

Though this may puzzle a theological college, no prison chaplain would need to explain it to his congregation, for our law reckons time on this same system. Though our legal day is a day and a night—twenty-four hours beginning at midnight—any part of a day counts as a day. Therefore, under a sentence of three days' imprisonment a prisoner is usually discharged on the morning of the third day, no matter how late on the first day he reaches the prison. Under such a sentence a prisoner is seldom more than forty hours in jail, and I have had official cognizance of cases where the detention was, in fact, only for thirty-three hours.

This mode of reckoning and of speaking was as familiar to the Jews as it is to our prison officials and those who frequent our criminal courts. In his *Horae Hebraicae*, Dr. John Lightfoot quotes the Jewish saying, "A day and a night make an *Onah*, and a part of an *Onah* is as the whole." And he adds, "Therefore, Christ may truly be said to have been in the grave three *Onoth*." To object that as Jonah was three days and three nights in the whale's belly, the Lord must have been in the grave for that full period is a transparent blunder; for, of course, the period intended in the Jonah narrative must be computed in accordance with "the dialect of the nation" (Lightfoot).

*Lest they should be converted, and I should heal them* (Matthew 13:15).

These words are misunderstood by many a Christian; and to not a few they are a real trouble. For they seem strangely out of keeping with the spirit of the Lord's ministry. But His words should always be studied in relation to their context and to the circumstances in which they were spoken. The "text-card system" of Bible study is a fruitful cause of misunderstanding and error.

During the early period of the Lord's ministry His words of grace and works of power were abundant, and they were open and free to all—witness the narrative of Matthew 4:23-25, a passage which attracts but little notice. It had been a time of noontide sunshine in the spiritual sphere, such as even that favored land had never experienced before. But the religious leaders of the people closed their eyes against the light; and, as Matthew 12:14 informs us, their hard-heartedness and hate culminated in their summoning a council to compass His destruction. And the latter section of that chapter records the awful words in which He pronounced their doom. Their day of visitation was over, and a sentence of spiritual blindness and deafness was pronounced upon them. From that time, therefore, His public teaching became veiled in parables (Matt. 13).

The change was so startling that the disciples came to Him with one accord to seek an explanation; and the passage from which the above words are taken gives His reply to their inquiries. Darkness was now to fall upon those who had despised the light.

But, as when darkness covered the land of Egypt, the Hebrews still had light, so was it here, for His parables were fully explained to the disciples.

The principle involved in this passage, therefore, is neither exceptional nor novel. Though the gospel amnesty which grace proclaims makes no exceptions, for divine grace has no limits, there are limits to the time within which the amnesty avails. And if sinners despise grace there is nothing for them but judgment, stern and inexorable. And the word goes forth, even in this age of grace, albeit judgment waits, "Ephraim is joined to idols; *let him alone* (Hos. 4:17)." This is an awfully solemn truth which explains the mystery of many a life.

> *The kingdom of heaven is like unto leaven which a woman took and hid in three measures of meal, till the whole was leavened* (Matthew 13:33).

The accepted interpretation of this parable takes the leaven to symbolize the good influence of Christianity in the world. It is admitted, however, even by the exponents of that view, that everywhere else in Scripture leaven is "symbolic of pollution and corruption." The question arises then, What meaning was the parable intended to convey to those who heard it? Having regard to the religious beliefs and deep-seated prejudices of the Jews, can there be any reasonable doubt as to the answer? Suppose that when the Lord had finished His teaching, some rabbi had explained to the hearers that the leaven in the parable represented a divine purifying agency, the amazement his words would have excited would have been such as a Christian con-

gregation today would feel if their minister—a staunch "teeto-
taller," withal—exemplified the spread of the gospel by the
"permeating influence" of a glass of brandy smuggled into the
family coffeepot!

"Smuggled," I say advisedly, for a specially significant word
in the parable is entirely ignored in the received exegesis. When
making bread in the course of her household duties, a woman
would naturally put leaven into the meal. But here the woman
*conceals* the leaven in the meal, the inference being an obvious
one, that she does it surreptitiously, and with a sinister purpose. Now a parable is defined by theologians as "a fictitious
story, invented to illustrate a truth." But why "fictitious"? "It
has been supposed that some of the parables narrate real and
not fictitious events." And if this very reasonable supposition
be well founded, a case may at that very time have engaged
public attention, where some evil woman had thus corrupted
the "three measures of meal" that had been set apart for an
offering.

But, it is urged, the alternative reading of the parable is vetoed on two grounds. First, by the very fact that the kingdom
of heaven is said to be like leaven, and therefore the leaven
must symbolize good and not evil. Here the theologians forget
their definition of a parable. For a parable must be read in its
entirety as presenting the truth which the Lord intends it to
teach. Were this remembered, Scripture would not be brought
into contempt by such trivia of exegesis as that the Good Sa-
maritan's two pence represent the two sacraments! or that, here,
the three measures of meal symbolize either "body, soul, and
spirit," or else "the descendants of the three sons of Noah"!
Tradition tells us that, from earliest times, this was the usual
amount of meal prepared for a baking (Gen. 18:6). It may have
been on this account that it was the quantity prescribed for a
meal-offering.

The second ground of veto is that the alternative reading of
the parable would make it conflict with the teaching of Scripture respecting the course and issue of this Christian dispensation. But so far from this being the case, it is in fact the accredited
exegesis of it which brings it into flagrant opposition to Scripture. Many a standard treatise might be cited in support of this

statement. But having regard to the space limits of this note, a single testimony must suffice, and it shall be that of a distinguished theologian who is an uncompromising champion of the "orthodox" exposition of the parable.

In his commentary on Matthew 12:43, Dean Alford, after explaining "the direct application of the passage to the Jewish people," writes as follows:

> Strikingly parallel with this runs the history of the Christian Church. Not long after the apostolic times, the golden calves of idolatry were set up by the church of Rome. What the effect of the captivity was to the Jews, that of the Reformation has been to Christendom. The first evil spirit has been cast out. But by the growth of hypocrisy, secularity, and rationalism, the house has become empty, swept, and garnished: swept and garnished by the decencies of civilization and discoveries of secular knowledge, but empty of living and earnest faith. And he must read prophecy but ill who does not see under all these seeming improvements the preparation for the final development of the man of sin, the great re-possession when idolatry and the seven worse spirits shall bring the outward frame of so-called Christendom to a fearful end.

Is it possible to reconcile Dean Alford's exposition of the leaven parable with these rich and solemn words about the long-drawn-out apostasy and coming doom of the professing Christian church?

*I will give unto thee [Peter] the keys of the kingdom of heaven* (Matthew 15:19).

But little need be added here to what has been said in the Introduction chapter about "the kingdom of heaven." The great apostasy which claims to be the keeper of Holy Scripture is so ignorant of Holy Writ that it confounds the kingdom of heaven with the church of this dispensation. The kingdom of heaven is the kingdom of Hebrew prophecy relating to earth and the earthly people of the covenant. And Peter was "the apostle of the circumcision." To him it was, therefore, that the Pentecostal proclamation to Israel was entrusted (Acts 2:22, 3:12). When "the word which God sent unto the children of Israel" was to be carried to Gentile proselytes, he was the appointed messenger (Acts 10:36). For among the Twelve Peter held the foremost place, and it was because there were twelve tribes of Israel that the apostles of the ministry were twelve in number (Matt. 19:28). Throughout what theologians call the Hebraic portion of the Acts, the apostle Peter is the foremost figure, and his ministry is preeminent. But Israel remained impenitent; and in the thirteenth chapter the apostles Paul and Barnabas were divinely "separated" to preach to the Gentiles, and the name of the apostle of the circumcision disappears from the narrative. In the first twelve chapters of Acts it occurs no less than fifty-six times, but, save in Acts 15:7, it is never found once in the last sixteen chapters of the book.

*There be some standing here which shall not see death till they see the Son of Man coming in His kingdom* (Matthew 15:28).

The following is the most approved exposition of this passage, and lest any one should suspect me of misstating a view which I reject, I give it in Dean Alford's words:

This declaration refers in its full meaning . . . to the destruction of Jerusalem, and the full manifestation of the kingdom of Christ by the annihilation of the Jewish polity.

Was there ever a more amazing example of "nightmare exegesis"? Did the disciples know that this was what they were asking for when they uttered the words the Lord had taught them, "Thy kingdom come"? They prayed that prayer with knowledge of the truth so plainly revealed in Scripture, that "the kingdom" would bring the *restoration* of the Jewish polity and relief from the Roman yoke. If, therefore, there be no other explanation of the passage open to us, let us humbly confess our ignorance, and leave it unexplained.

But before we yield to a "counsel of despair" let us clear our minds of all preconceptions, and study afresh the whole passage from 15:28 to 17:8. And reading it unbroken by the chapter division, let us consider whether it does not afford us the solution we seek.

Most great commentators agree that the Lord was pointing

to some definite event which would occur during the lifetime of some of His disciples. But they urge, not without some show of reason, that the words "shall not taste of death" imply a somewhat remote event. Suppose, then, we omit these words, and read the passage thus, "Verily I say unto you, there are some standing here who shall see the Son of Man coming in His kingdom." Should we need the words of 2 Peter 1:16-18 to convince us that it was fulfilled at the Transfiguration?

There was one other event, and only one, in the life of the disciples which might claim consideration if a drastic "spiritualizing" of the Lord's language could be allowed, namely, the Day of Pentecost. But that would leave equally unexplained the words above omitted. The question remains, therefore, how can they be accounted for? I would answer boldly that if we must make a choice between leaving this difficulty unsolved and adopting an unscriptural "nightmare" exegesis of the passage, we shall do well to adopt the former alternative. I venture to suggest, however, that we might possibly find a very simple solution of it if we knew what was working in the minds of the disciples at the time.

Certain statements in the Gospels indicate that they were "dull of hearing" about much of the Lord's teaching. And if they treated the truth of the kingdom in its spiritual aspect in the manner that most of us now treat the truth of His coming, relegating it to the sphere of mere doctrine and sentiment, may not the above omitted words have been a graciously veiled rebuke?

It would be easy to offer many a plausible suggestion respecting the Lord's purpose in speaking thus. But while we may freely attempt to analyze the thoughts of the disciples in such a case, any speculating about what was passing in the mind of our divine Lord would be to tread on sacred ground.

I must not fail to notice yet another exposition of our verse; but I notice it only for reprobation, although it is sanctioned by some eminent authorities. It is that the Lord was here referring to "His *ultimate* glorious coming." This view solves the question above discussed by rejecting the "difficult words" of the verse as being absolutely untrue. Such passages as Mark 13:32 and Acts 1:7 explain why the Lord refused to specify "times and seasons," and seeing that in the case before us He definitely fixed a time limit, the fulfillment of His words could have no reference to "times and season," or, in other words, to events foretold in prophecy. The proposed exegesis, moreover, betrays strange neglect of Scripture. For it is certain that the "ultimate glorious coming" will be long ages after "the coming of the Son of Man in His kingdom"—a thousand years at least. And some would tell us that here "a thousand years" is an abstract term to mean an indefinitely vast era of time.

*Go and sell all that thou hast, and give to the poor* (Matthew 19:21) (Mark 10:21; Luke 18:22).

If we are Christ's disciples, why do we not act on this? the infidel mockingly demands. And our answer is plain: because it is not addressed to us. The Lord knows each heart and each life, and He deals with each in infinite wisdom. Another man, we read, besought the Lord for permission to follow Him, but "Return to thine own house" was the Lord's answer to his appeal (Luke 8:38, 39). And Lazarus of Bethany, whom the Lord loved, had "possessions"; but instead of telling him to part with them, the Lord became his guest. And in the case of the apostle Peter, so far from desiring him to sell his house in Capernaum, the Lord made His home there.

God "has no pleasure in fools (Eccl. 5:4)." And to take every word of Scripture to one's self, irrespective of the circumstances in which it was spoken, is to be a very mischievous kind of fool; for such folly brings discredit upon Holy Writ. Our answer to the infidel, then, is that Scripture teaches us that a Christian who, having others dependent on him, sells all that he has and gives it to the poor, "has denied the faith, and is worse than an infidel" (1 Tim. 5:8).

But is not "community of goods" enjoined by Acts 4:34-37? Assuredly not. The apostle's words to Ananias (5:4) make it clear that the disciples were under no obligation to part with their "possessions." Their doing so was a "freewill offering." And the passage is misread because the distinctive character of that brief Pentecostal dispensation is ignored. It was a waiting time.

"During the last Carlist rising in Spain a wealthy Marquis was said to have mortgaged his estate, and to have thrown the proceeds into the war-chest of the insurrection. It was a reasonable act on the part of any one who believed in the success of the Pretender's cause." And the Hebrew disciples of Pentecostal days were living in the hopes inspired by the prophecy and promise recorded in Acts 3:19-21.

*For many be called, but few chosen* (Matthew 20:16).

Intelligent students of Scripture take note of the first occurrence of important words. And in this verse we have the first occurrence of the word "elect." The striking fact that the Lord here uses it with reference, not to salvation, but to service, may cause surprise to many, but not to those who have studied the use of the word in the Greek version of the Hebrew Scriptures, which, as we know, exercised a very marked influence upon the language of the New Testament. For in most, if not all, of its occurrences in the Septuagint it is used to express excellence and appreciation.[3]

The first is in Genesis 23:6. In response to Abraham's appeal for a burial-place for Sarah, the children of Heth replied, "In *the best* of our sepulchers bury thy dead." It is used again six times in Genesis: four times of *choice* cattle, and twice of *choice* ears of corn (chap. 41). Its first occurrence in a higher sense is its application to Joshua in Numbers 11:28 (where the LXX reading is "the chosen one"). And in Isaiah 28:16 it is stamped with its highest value by its application to the Lord Himself (cf. 1 Peter 2:6).

"Words are the counters of wise men, the money of fools"; and a word may, in one connection, stand for gold, and, in another, for some coin of inferior metal. But expositors are apt to forget this, and to treat the counters as though they were coins. This has had deplorable results in relation to the parable which ends with our present verse. Not only does it rob us of important teaching and solemn warning respecting the Lord's service, but it operates as a flagrant denial of the truth of the

---

3. The passages are given in the author's book, *The Entail of the Covenant.*

gospel. The parable does not describe the case of the man who sends out his servants to bring in the destitute to the banquet which his invited guests have despised (Luke 14:16-22); but of the householder who goes out to hire laborers to work in his vineyard. And every man he hires receives the wages promised him; but it is only some of them who earn special appreciation and approval. Mark the order and significance of the words: many are *klêtoi*, but few are *eklektoi*. According to our ordinary use of the word, all were "chosen," for that is implied in the hiring. But here the "choosing" is at the end of the day's labor. Are we, then, to conclude that the divine decree which fixes our eternal destiny awaits, and is dependent upon, the value of our service?

Embedded in this parable there are some most important truths that we are prone to forget. The fact that it is the householder himself who hires the laborers points to a truth which is enforced in many a Scripture—the truth, namely, that although God entrusts to His servants the duty of seeking the lost, and bidding them to the banquet of salvation, the call to service is His own prerogative.

No less clear is the teaching of the parable for those who are called to labor in the Lord's vineyard. As we know from other Scriptures, it is "the service of *sons*," and not, as some would tell us, of sinners on probation, whose eternal destiny will depend on the character and value of their service. And we must not confound "the judgment seat of Christ" with "the great white throne." Not that the issue of either judgment will be the eternal destiny of men—*that* will be manifested by the resurrection; and yet both have to do with our earthly life, "the things done in the body" (2 Cor. 5:10) or "the things written in the books" (Rev. 20:12).

But, I repeat, it is to laborers in the vineyard that this parable specially refers. And the question at issue will be whether the laborer will be *eklektos*, or, as the alternative, *adokimos* (to use the Apostle's word in 1 Corinthians 9:27). However, any exposition which treats either the Lord's parable or the apostle's warning words as though they referred to the eternal salvation, or the eternal doom, of men, not only perverts these Scriptures, but betrays ignorance or neglect of the great truth of salvation by grace through faith.

*This generation shall not pass, till all these things be fulfilled* (Matthew 24:34).

This is a favorite verse with the rationalists, for in their ignorance they cite it as discrediting Holy Scripture. Is it not clear, they ask, that the Lord's words have failed? Here is Dean Alford's interpretation of it:

> It may be well to show that *genea* has in Hellenistic Greek the meaning of a race or family of people. See Jeremiah 8:3, 70. Compare Matthew 23:36 with verse 35 . . . 'This generation' did not slay Zacharias—so that the whole people are addressed. See also chapter 12:45, in which the meaning absolutely requires this sense.

He further cites chapter 17:17; Luke 16:8 and 17:25; Acts 11:40; Philippians 2:15. And he adds, "In all these places *genea* is *genos*, or nearly so."

Some scholars explain the passage by reference to the fact that the word rendered "this" may with equal correctness be translated "that." Thus the statement would mean that the same generation which sees the setting up of the abomination of desolations (v. 15) will see all these things come to pass.

Our only difficulty, therefore, in interpreting it is that it involves our adjudicating between alternative solutions which are equally satisfactory and equally scholarly.

*Then shall the kingdom of heaven be likened unto ten virgins* (Matthew 25:1).

"How [it is asked] is the kingdom of heaven like ten virgins?" The question exemplifies a popular, but very erroneous, mode of reading the parables. As the dictionary tells us, a parable is "a story of something which might have happened, told to illustrate some doctrine, or to make some duty clear." To understand the parable aright, therefore, we must study it as a whole, and with reference to the particular doctrine or duty it is designed to teach. And in this case the thirteenth verse leaves no doubt as to its intention—"Watch therefore, for ye know neither the day nor the hour wherein the Son of Man cometh (Matt. 25:13)."

But this parable is too often read without noticing the em-

phatic word with which it begins: "*Then*—at the period spoken
of at the end of the last chapter, namely, the coming of the Lord
to His personal reign—not at His final coming to judgment"
(Alford). To be still more accurate and explicit, it is the Lord's
coming as "Son of Man"—an event which is later in time, and
wholly distinct from, the Coming which is the special hope of
the Christian in this Christian age. "The hope of the church," to
use Bengel's phrase, is a "mystery" truth which was not revealed
until Israel was set aside.

> *Go ye therefore, and make disciples of all the nations, baptizing
> them into the name of the Father and of the Son and of the
> Holy Ghost* (Matthew 28:19, R.V.).

The closing passages of the four Gospels have always been a
difficulty with theologians, and often a cause of perplexity to
Christians generally. And it is about the last five verses of Matthew that the difficulties chiefly cluster. Indeed to any one who
is dependent on our Authorized Version they seem over-
whelming. For the chapter seems to record the fact that after
the Resurrection the eleven disciples forthwith left Jerusalem
for the appointed meeting place in Galilee, and there received
the parting commands of their risen Lord. But this, of course, is
entirely inconsistent with the narratives of Luke and John. Dean
Alford here speaks of "the imperfect and fragmentary nature
of the materials out of which our narrative is built." But the
idea is absurd that any one of the apostles could, to his dying
day, forget the Lord's appearing to them on the evening of the
resurrection, and again after eight days. But if on five different
occasions our Lord appeared to a company of His disciples,
how is it that this evangelist records but one? Why does Matthew ignore the Lord's appearings to His gathered disciples in
Jerusalem? This is but part of a wider question: Why does the
first Gospel ignore Jerusalem altogether, so far as it is possible
to ignore it, in the record of our Lord's ministry?

The purpose of the Gospel of Matthew in the divine scheme
of revelation is to present Christ as Israel's Messiah. And Galilee
was prophetically and dispensationally associated with the
godly remnant which, in the apostasy of the nation, was di-

vinely regarded as the true Israel. Therefore is it that the Lord's ministry in Galilee has such prominence in this gospel. According to Matthew the last words spoken to the Eleven before the agony in Gethsemane were, that after He was risen again He would go before them into Galilee (26:32). And the first message sent to His brethren after the resurrection, first by the mouth of the angel who appeared to the women at the sepulcher, and afterwards by His own lips, was that He would meet them in Galilee (28:7, 10).

What, then, is needed to complete the book? If unchecked by the Spirit of God, the apostle would doubtless have given a record of the events of those forty days. It is idle to talk of "fragmentary materials." Any one of the disciples could have compiled such a narrative, but it would have been wholly foreign to the scope and purpose of the first gospel. As it is the Galilee ministry which is the burden of it, all that remains is to record how, in the scene of that ministry, the Lord gathered His disciples round Him, and gave them those enriching and intensely prophetic words with which that gospel closes.

But who were the disciples thus addressed? It is rightly assumed that this was the occasion when our Lord appeared to above five hundred brethren at once. If it was not here, then this, the most important event of the forty days, is unnoticed in the Gospels, which is an incredible supposition. The message from the sepulcher will throw light on this. As the Lord intended to meet the Eleven that very evening, why should He send them a command to go into Galilee? And, as He was about to reveal Himself to Peter, why should the women be made the bearers of such a message? Is it not obvious that the message was intended for the whole company of the disciples?

Let us now consider verses 16 and 17. "Then the eleven disciples went away into Galilee, into a mountain where Jesus had appointed them; and when they saw Him they worshiped Him: but some doubted." Read by itself, the narrative seems clear and simple; but read in the light of what other gospels tell us, it seems misleading and false. But the error is suggested by the English rendering of the text. The first word of the sixteenth verse appears to be emphatic, whereas it is not in the original at all. The word rendered "then" in the Authorized Version and "but" in the R.V. is what the grammarians call "the *de* resumptive," which is often untranslatable, and sometimes untranslated. In the first verse of this chapter, for instance, it is ignored; for the mere fact that the verse is made the beginning of a new chapter conveys to the English reader much the same sense that the use of the particle in question does in Greek. And so here. The sixteenth verse begins a new paragraph, and it might fitly begin a new chapter. It is not a continuation of a consecutive narrative, but the record of a special event. "The eleven disciples went into Galilee, into the mountain where Jesus had appointed them. "

But why the *eleven* disciples, if above five hundred brethren went to the meeting place? The reason is not doubtful. The apostle's words in 1 Corinthians 15:6 indicate plainly that the appearing to the five hundred brethren was a matter of general knowledge in the church. No less so was the fact that "the eleven" remained in Jerusalem after the main company of the disciples had gone to Galilee. That they were expressly enjoined to remain in Jerusalem until the fulfillment of "the promise of the Father," and that they still remained in Jerusalem when the church was scattered by the Stephen persecution—these also, doubtless, were well-known facts, the public property of all the believers. What wonder, then, if the apostle should record with emphasis that "the eleven disciples went into Galilee." That the rest were there was a fact well known to all; but that the Eleven were present needed to be placed on record.

To the English reader this mention of the Eleven seems to lend prominence to the "theys" in the following sentence: "And when they saw Him, they worshiped." But the pronouns are not in the Greek. To say, "And when He was seen He was worshiped" would express the meaning of the original better than a stricter translation. It must be conceded, however, that even when thus rendered the words must be taken as referring to the Eleven, unless we assume that there is an omitting of words in the sentence of which they form a part. But such an omitting of words is precisely what we should expect if the fact that five hundred brethren were present was a matter of common knowledge, and the writer had the fact vividly before his mind when he wrote.

This suggestion is in a striking way confirmed by the statement that some doubted. That after the Lord's rebuking Thomas for doubting before even he had seen Him, any of the Eleven still doubted even while they looked upon Him—this cannot be tolerated for a moment. It is certain, therefore, that others were present. But what others? Are we to suppose, I again ask, that such an event as our Lord's appearing to above five hundred brethren at once is unnoticed in the Gospels? Are we to suppose that the appearing recorded in Matthew was unnoticed by Paul in summing up the evidences for the resurrection? When it was a question of marshalling the proofs of the resurrection, the fact that five hundred brethren were present became of principal importance. But here it was wholly immaterial. That to His gathered disciples, the Eleven being of the number, He gave the great Commission—this was all that was essential. To accept the blunder theory, or the fragmentary and imperfect materials theory, is to stultify ourselves. In whatever way we approach the matter, we are drawn toward the same conclusion, namely, that the Gospel of Matthew, ignoring all that is beyond the divine purpose for which it is written, closes the narrative of the Galilee ministry by recording the Lord's appearing to His assembled disciples in the scene of that ministry, and His Commission to them to evangelize the world.

Another difficulty claims brief notice in conclusion, namely, the fact that this Commission was never acted on. Its terms are definite. But no less definite are the facts. "Make disciples of all the nations[4] baptizing them." And yet, even when the church was scattered by the Stephen persecution, the apostles remained in Jerusalem; and the scattered disciples preached "to none but unto the Jews only" (Acts 8:1, 11:19). Not even did the apostle to the Gentiles act on it; as witness his emphatic statement, "He sent me not to baptize" (1 Cor. 1:17).

A special vision was needed to lead Peter to visit the house of Cornelius. And at the Jerusalem Council of Acts 15 not one of the inspired apostles was led to refer to this Commission. Indeed the Book of Acts contains no reference to it whatever.

---

4. In Scripture "the nations" always means the Gentile nations. It is an ignorant false interpretation to construe the term as including Israel.

The difficulty is insoluble if we ignore the scope and character of Matthew's gospel. But in common with so much of the teaching of that gospel, "the Great Commission" pertains dispensationally to the future age of the kingdom of heaven, when the Lord shall be King over all the earth; and all people, nations, and languages shall serve Him. And when that day comes, the question will not be of individual faith in an absent and rejected Savior and Lord, but rather of national submission to divine sovereignty openly declared and enforced on earth. And baptism will become the outward and visible sign of that submission. Now we can understand why it is to the Gentiles that the messengers are sent, blessing to Israel being assumed. For the redeemed of this dispensation will have passed to heaven, and the true remnant of Israel, typified by the little company that gathered round the Lord upon the mountain, will be the missionaries to the world. In contemplation of it the apostle exclaimed, "If the casting away of them be the reconciling of the world, what shall the receiving of them be, but life from the dead?" (Rom. 11:15).[5]

*And they brought young children to Him, that He should touch them: and the disciples rebuked those that brought them* (Mark 10:13; Matthew 19:13; Luke 18:15).

This is one of the most popular passages in the Gospels; for sacred art has portrayed the scene as described in sacred literature—the mothers crowding round the Lord, with their little ones at their skirts, and the disciples trying to keep them back. But the picture is false to fact. No devout Jew would have barred a child's approach to a Rabbi; and that the disciples should have acted in this way is quite incredible, so recent was that wonderful incident at Capernaum—presumably in the apostle Peter's home—when the Lord called a little child to Him, and taking him up in His arms, gave utterance to these never-to-be-forgotten words, "It is not the will of your Father who is in heaven, that one of these little ones should perish" (Matt. 18:2, 14; cf. Mark 9:33, 36).

---

5. The Bible student will here turn to passages such as, for example, Dan. 7:13, 14; Zech. 14; and the many kingdom Psalms, such as 96-100.

The evangelist Luke's narrative explains the disciples' action; for it tells us that the women "were bringing *even their babies* to Him,"[6] and this seemed an unwarrantable intrusion. The word *brephos* means primarily an unborn child, and then, as here, a child newly born. It has no other meaning in Greek. It was their newborn infants that these godly mothers brought to the Lord Jesus. And their faith and devotion won for them far more than they ventured to ask of Him. Their appeal was that He would *touch* them; and not only did He put His hands upon them, but "He took them up in His arms and blessed them." What a Scripture to stir the heart of a Christian mother as she holds her newborn infant in her arms! And the Capernaum words are well-fitted to strengthen and guide her faith as her little ones gather round her in the nursery.

No truth of Scripture has suffered more from the teaching of the Latin Fathers than this about "the little ones." But though heaven and earth shall pass away, the words the Lord Jesus spoke on earth shall never pass away. Let us then accept these words unperverted and unobscured by Augustinian doctrine: "It is not the will of your Father who is in heaven, that one of these little ones should perish." And under the microscope they stand out all the clearer; for "the form of the proposition has all the force that belongs to the rhetorical negative . . . namely, that the will of the Father is the very opposite of that."[7]

*He said, Weep not; she is not dead, but sleepeth* (Luke 8:49-56; Matthew 9: 23-25; Mark 5:38ff.).

The commonly accepted exegesis of this passage about Jairus' daughter presents a strange problem. The Lord declared with emphatic definiteness that Jairus' child was *not* dead; but the crowd of mourners "laughed Him to scorn," for they knew better! And Christian expositors reject the Lord's explicit testimony and accept that of the mocking Jews!

Jairus had fallen at the Lord's feet, beseeching Him to come to his house; but, their progress being much delayed (Matt.

---

6. To render *kai* by "also" in this sentence makes it entirely meaningless. And (as Bloomfield notices) the article before *brephê* has the force of *"their* babies."

7. Bishop Ellicott, *New Testament Commentary.* The subject of this note is the burden of the author's book, *The Entail of the Covenant.*

9:42-48), they were met by tidings that the child was dead. Thereupon the Lord intervened with the assurance, "She will recover." Thus it is the R.V. renders the word in John 11:12, when the disciples said of Lazarus, "If he is fallen asleep, he will recover." It is the word the Lord had used in verse 48 to "the woman with the issue of blood," and the same word that is translated "healed" in verse 36. In its 106 occurrences in the New Testament the word is very often used of saving from death, but never once in the sense of raising the dead.

"Has fallen asleep" is a familiar euphemism for "has died"; but to use that phrase to deny the reality of death would be to utter a flagrant untruth; and yet this is what is here attributed to the Lord Jesus! A reference to John 11:11-14 will exemplify this. "Lazarus has fallen asleep," the Lord said to the disciples; but when they mistook His meaning, "He said unto them plainly, Lazarus has died."

But in marked contrast with this, the Lord had said that Jairus' daughter "would recover" (v. 50). And when He entered the house, and before He saw the child, He announced in the confidence of divine knowledge, "She has not died, but she is sleeping."

And then, standing by her bedside, He took her by the hand, saying, "Maid, arise" (or "wake up"). And, the narrative adds, "her spirit came again"— the identical words used in the Greek Bible to describe Samson's recovery as recorded in Judges 15:19.

But, it will be said, the universally accepted reading of this passage must surely have some different and surer basis. Not so; it rests entirely upon two grounds. First, the presumption that the facts of the case must have been better known to the Jewish mourners than to the Lord of glory! And secondly, that as the Lord meant that Lazarus was dead when He said that he was sleeping, His word about Jairus' child must be understood in the same sense. This is worthy of the Sunday school! For the word He used in John 11:11 is altogether different from the word He here employed. In all but four of its eighteen occurrences His Lazarus word (*koimaō*) signifies death; whereas the word He here used (*katheudō*) never bears that meaning in any of its twenty-one occurrences in the New Testament.[8]

---

8. ˙ In 1 Thessalonians 5:10, the word must, of course, have the same meaning as in verses 6 and 7.

And yet if the Lord had really said, "She is not dead, but sleepeth," some might still plead for putting a mystical meaning on the phrase. But the words He actually used, "She did not die" (*ou gar apethanen*), were a definite and unequivocal statement of a fact. And His hearers were clearly intended to understand them thus. There was no element of dramatic effect in any of the Lord's miracles. And knowing that the child, though past recovery, was still alive, He who was "the truth" would not have it supposed that He was raising her from the dead.[9] But by a word He restored her to full health and vigor (v. 55). The reality of the miracle is not in question, nor yet its testimony to His divine power. But among honorable men the test of truth is the meaning which words are intended to convey to others; are we then to attribute a lower standard of truthfulness to the language of our divine Lord? For this is involved in so reading His words, "She did not die," that an elaborate and subtle argument is needed to vindicate their truth. This is the question here at issue.

*Strive to enter in at the strait gate* (Luke 13:24).

This text is very generally misunderstood; partly through misreading its principal word, and partly through ignorance of Oriental customs. The imagery is not the same as that of Matthew 7:13. In one of the two leaves of an Eastern city gate there was a small narrow door which was open to foot-passengers for a while after the main gate was closed at sundown.[10] And the false interpretation of our commentaries is that "Strive to enter in" means to struggle as a wrestler struggles. If any one had offered such a suggestion to an audience of Orientals, they would have turned away with feelings either of amusement or of pity, for his ignorance. For a belated traveler who tried to enter in that fashion would have been taken for an enemy or a lunatic, and either cut down or thrown out! And such an exposition of the words is remarkably opposed to the doctrine and the spirit of the Gospel.

---

9. For the same reason, doubtless, He charged the parents to tell no one about the miracle (v. 56)—a charge they seem to have disregarded (Matt. 9:26).

10. James Neil, *Everyday Life in the Holy Land.*

This, no doubt, is the primary meaning of the word *agonizo-mai*, and it is so used in some other passages. But it is not its only meaning. In Colossians 14:12, for example, the apostle uses it to describe the fervent earnestness of Epaphras' prayers for his Colossian brethren. And so here. It is one of the Lord's many warnings against trifling with God or with eternal interests. No Oriental would have missed its meaning. The wayfarer knows that, though the sun has set, the "narrow gate" is still open; so there is no need to hurry. Then why not linger here, or turn aside there? But although God looks for no merit of any kind in us, He must not be treated as we would not dare to treat a fellow-man. "Behold, *now* is the day of salvation" is His word: "not now, but *tomorrow*" is the response of the human heart.

As we study the sequel, we must distinguish between the dispensational bearing of the Lord's words and their general application. No Oriental would miss His meaning when the allegory of "the narrow gate" merges in that of the feast to which invitations have been issued with Eastern prodigality. And the guests have no need to knock, for the door stands open. But once the master of the house "is risen up and has shut the door," neither knocking nor pleading will avail. For Israel that crisis was at hand—their day of visitation was far spent.

And now, in the sequel, the Lord gives an explicit answer to the question which called forth these solemn words of warning. The saved will *not* be few. Outcast sinners will come from every point of the compass, and sit down in the kingdom with Abraham, and Isaac, and Jacob, while the favored people who boast of their descent from these patriarchs will be themselves "thrust out."

Such, then, is the primary interpretation of the passage. But it has a very special application to ourselves in this Christian age. And here the error of the received exegesis is still more apparent. The little entrance door in an Eastern city gate was not only narrow, it was so low that a man had to stoop when passing in. But there was no difficulty of any kind in entering, if only he bowed his head, and had no pack to carry. What imagery could possibly describe more aptly how a sinner must come to Christ! And our present verse is not so much a command as a gracious appeal and invitation, given in the spirit of the Savior's words in the last two verses of the chapter.[11]

### *And the lord commended the unjust steward* (Luke 16:8).

No chapter in the Gospels is more misread than the sixteenth of Luke. The commonly accepted version of it may be summarized as follows: "A certain rich man had an agent who was accused of robbing him; so he gave him notice of dismissal. The steward then set himself to rob him more flagrantly than ever; and his master commended him for his cleverness."

Did a rustic preacher ever propound anything sillier or more harmful to a company of yokels! And suppose, to make matters worse, he followed it up by a sermon with the moral: "Woe to the rich: blessed are the poor!" Yet this deplorable folly and error is attributed to our divine Lord!

In this group of parables we have a series of exquisite pictures, drawn by the hand of the Master, to illustrate the great life-choice. In the prodigal son we have the case of one who "wasted" his own "portion of goods" in selfish and sinful pleasure, but afterwards repented, and was restored. In the steward we have the case of one who wasted his employer's "goods" by waste and neglect; but who repented, and was forgiven. And in the rich man in the last parable of the series we have one who persistently lived for this world, and died impenitent.

The steward was "unrighteous" in the sense that he was a careless, easy-going man, who "let things slide," leaving debts uncollected, and allowing accounts to run on. Thus it was that he was "wasting" his master's property. It was a case, not of occasional acts of dishonesty, but of habitual carelessness. His dishonesty was of a passive kind. And what earned for him his master's praise was his action when brought to be judged, and dishonesty of any kind was no longer possible.

Instead of alienating the debtors by enforcing immediate payment in full, he set himself to win their friendship by giving them a most liberal discount, and at his own expense, of course;

---

11. See note on Matthew 7:13, *ante*.

for now he was working under strict observation. And he did this in order that, when he lost his office, they might receive him into their houses.

*This is the whole point of the parable.* Its lesson is not that roguery succeeds, or is commendable in any way, but as the Lord Himself explains it by the words, "Make to yourselves friends by means of the mammon of unrighteousness, that when it shall fail ye may be received into the eternal tabernacles." The moral of the parable is the wisdom of using the present in view of the future; of living in a world that is "passing away," under the influence of that other world which is abiding and eternal. It is the application in the highest sphere of a principle which is recognized by "the children of this world." For the successful man is one who has learned to make "today" subordinate to "tomorrow," and to forego a present advantage in order to secure a prospective gain.

To enforce this still more plainly, the Lord went on to say, "If ye have not been faithful in that which is another's, who will give you that which is your own?" As the parable is usually read, these words seem inexplicable. But their meaning is clear: spiritual gifts are our own, but the mammon is entrusted to us as stewards. How false, then, is the prevailing belief that, in the Christian life, the "religious" and the "secular" are in separate compartments. The Christian is as really God's servant in the one sphere as in the other.

And then verse 13 gives the final lesson. The Christian is to use the world; but if he uses it excessively it becomes his master. And though mammon be a good servant, it is an evil master. Moreover, "No servant can serve two masters . . . Ye cannot serve God and mammon." We must choose between them. And the concluding parable about Dives and Lazarus is given to guide our choice.[12]

*Behold the Lamb of God, which taketh away the sin of the world* (John 1:29).

---

12. These parables are dealt with in the author's work, *The Way: Chapters on the Christian Life.*

This rendering of the text in both our versions savors of exegesis. John the Baptist's words are definitely clear, "Behold the Lamb of God, who is bearing the sin of the world." And they are usually supposed to be a revelation to the Jews that Christ was to die; the only question in doubt being whether the type to which they refer be the Paschal lamb or the sin-offering.

But this involves a glaring anachronism. For it was not until the Sanhedrin decreed His destruction (Matt. 12:32) that the Lord revealed even to the Twelve that He was to be put to death. And so utterly opposed was it to all Jewish beliefs and hopes that they gave no heed to it. Upon other grounds also such an exegesis is unintelligent. For the Passover did not typify "bearing sin," and a lamb was never the sin-offering victim. Nor was it "the sin of the world" that the scapegoat bore away, but the sins of the children of Israel (Lev. 16:21).

"Who is bearing the sin of the world." This was not a prophecy of Calvary, but a revelation of what the Lord was during His life. Therefore the word here used is not a sacrificial term, as in 1 Peter 2:24 and other kindred passages, but an ordinary word in common use for taking up and carrying burdens. Its five occurrences in John 5:8-12 are fairly representative of its use in the ninety-six other passages where it is found. Accordingly we read in 1 John 3:5—the only other passage where the word is used in this connection—"He was manifested to take away [or to bear] sins" (R.V.), the apostle's purpose being, as the context plainly indicates, not to assert the doctrine of expiation, but to impress on the saints that sin is utterly opposed to Christ, and hinders fellowship with Him. Mark the word "manifested"; it was not the mystery of Calvary, but the openly declared purpose of His life. For in this sense He was a sin-bearer during all His earthly sojourn; as witness, for example, His groans and tears at the grave of Lazarus. He took up and bore the burden of human sin; not as to its guilt—*that* was not till Gethsemane and Calvary— but as to the sufferings and sorrows it brought upon humanity.

"He was oppressed, yet He humbled Himself and opened not His mouth; as a lamb that is led to the slaughter, and as a sheep that before her shearers is dumb, yea He opened not His mouth" (Isaiah 53:7, R.V.). There is a general consensus of opinion that to this passage it is that John the Baptist's words refer. And it is noteworthy that it contains no sacrificial language; for, in the Hebrew, "slaughter" is a common word that points to the shambles. It foretold the Messiah's earthly life of humiliation and suffering. And this it was that the Jews could not understand, and would not accept. Hence the force and meaning of John the Baptist's inspired words uttered at the very threshold of the ministry.

Let no one suppose then that the foregoing exposition disparages the truth of the expiation accomplished upon Calvary. That great truth rests upon a foundation too firm and sure to need support from a misreading of John the Baptist's testimony. Indeed, it is the accepted exegesis of the passage that imperils that truth. For it affords a colorable justification for the profane heresy that during the Lord's earthly ministry He rested under the cloud of separation from His Father (see note on 1 Peter 2:24). To form too high an estimate of the death of Christ would be impossible, but it is a deplorable fact that the prolonged martyrdom of His earthly life has far too little place in our thoughts.

> *Except a man be born of water and the Spirit, he cannot enter the kingdom of God* (John 3:5).

The fact that the traditional view of this passage, which connects it with Christian baptism, is rejected by a weighty minority of theologians, from Calvin to Bishop John C. Ryle, should make us ready to consider the matter with an open mind. And Dr. Ryle's "six reasons" for rejecting it, enumerated in his *Expository Thoughts on the Gospels*, might well make an end of controversy on the subject. Indeed, the traditional view is vetoed by the glaring anachronism it involves. For Christian baptism had not then been instituted, and even the disciples themselves knew nothing of it. And yet the Lord indignantly rebuked Nicodemus for not understanding His words about a birth by water and the Spirit. "Art thou the teacher of Israel [He exclaimed] and I knowest not these things?" (John 3:10). It is certain, therefore, that He was referring to some Old Testament Scripture with which a rabbi of the Sanhedrin ought to have been familiar. The only answer to this is the profane suggestion that the Lord's solemn words had reference to the Jewish baptism of proselytes, a purely human ordinance, which the Jews in days of apostasy derived from ancient paganism. We must avoid the error suggested by our Authorized Version that the words imply a twofold birth, of water and of the Spirit. For in the next verse, and again in verse 8, the water is omitted, and the new man is said to be "born of the Spirit." And this rules out the false meaning that the Lord was referring to "the baptism of John," for that baptism was expressly contrasted with the Spirit's work (Matt. 3:11). It was a confession of failure and sin, to prepare for receiving a Messiah whose near advent John the Baptist proclaimed. Christian baptism, on the other hand, was a confession of faith in Christ already come, and gone back to heaven; and of submission to Him as their Lord, on the part of those who professed to have been already born of the Spirit. Therefore, when the household of Cornelius were brought in, their baptism was not the new birth, but a public recognition that they had been already born of water and the Spirit. For the question was, "Can any man forbid water that these should not be baptized *who have received the Holy Spirit* as well as we?"

Baptism is a public act performed by man, for which man can fix the day and hour. The new birth of water and the Spirit is altogether the work of God; and as our Lord so expressly declares, no man can forecast, no man can command it. "The Spirit breathes where He wills, and thou hearest His voice, but knowest not whence He cometh and whither He goeth: so is every one that is born of the Spirit (John 3:8)." It was presumably the obvious reference to Ezekiel's prophecy which led our translators to render *pneuma* by "wind." Of course, it may have that meaning; but the word occurs 370 times in the New Testament (23 times in John), and yet nowhere else is it so translated. And the word rendered "sound" is *phônê*, the ordinary word for "voice," and it is so translated in 130 of its 139 occurrences.

But the need of all this discussion arises from the accumulations of error and prejudice which obscure the teaching of the passage. In added words the Lord Himself made His meaning unequivocally clear. In verse 9 Nicodemus repeats as a humble seeker after truth the question which he had previously raised (v. 4) in petulant unbelief, "How can a man be born anew?" And now the answer is given to him: "As Moses lifted up the serpent in the wilderness, even so must the Son of Man be lifted up, that whosoever believeth in Him should not perish, but have eternal life." It was not as the result of a mystical human rite that Nicodemus was to be born again, but by believing in Christ "lifted up" (cf. 8:28 and 12:32). And, as other Scriptures tell us, "Faith cometh by hearing, and hearing by the Word of God (Rom. 10:17)." "We are born again by the living and eternally-abiding Word of God" (1 Peter 1:23).

In this matter Christendom is in direct conflict with Scripture. Christendom teaches that baptism symbolizes *birth*. Holy Scripture declares that it symbolizes *death*. Christendom teaches that it is the putting away of the filth of the flesh. Holy Scripture declares "it is not the putting away of the filth of the flesh, but the answer of a good conscience toward God." And in the same passage (1 Peter 3:21) the apostle enforces the symbolism of death, by referring to baptism as an antitype of the Flood. The water which overwhelmed the world bore up the ark. Noah was thus saved from death by death, as is the sinner who, on believing in Christ, becomes one with Him in death. But if it be a question of the new birth, "we are born again by the Word of God."

As already noticed, the Lord's words to Nicodemus referred to some Old Testament Scripture with which he ought to have been familiar. Nor is there any doubt what that Scripture was, namely, Ezekiel 36 – 37 a prophecy that was greatly cherished by the Jew; and ignorance of it would have been as discreditable to a rabbi as ignorance of the Nicodemus sermon would be to a Christian theologian.

There we read, "I will sprinkle clean water upon you . . . . And I will put My Spirit within you" (Ezek. 36:25-27). And in chapter 37 we have the vision of the valley of dry bones, when the prophet is told to call upon the dry bones to "hear the word of the Lord"; and to prophesy to the Spirit to breathe upon them. The water of Ezekiel's prophecy was "the water of purification" of Numbers 19. Water which had flowed over the ashes of the sin-offering had efficacy to cleanse the sinner. And the antitype of that water is the Word of God by which we are born again (1 Peter 1:23). When, therefore, the Lord went on to tell Nicodemus of eternal life through faith in Him as lifted up upon the cross (v. 14), He was unfolding the meaning of that Ezekiel prophecy, and of the type to which, as every Rabbi recognized, it so clearly referred.

To recapitulate. In Scripture, baptism symbolizes *death*, which is the very antithesis of birth; and it is never associated with regeneration.[13] And, as Bishop Ryle notices in his *Expository Thoughts*, "there is little about baptism in the Epistles." How then did it come to signify regeneration, and to acquire such prominence in Christendom religion? The *Hibbert Lectures*, 1888, by Dr. Edwin Hatch, of Oxford (Vice-Principal of St. Mary Hall), supplies a clear and conclusive answer to this question. The early church in its apostasy was so thoroughly corrupted by Greek paganism that, in respect of baptism, it adopted not only the doctrines and ritual, but the very terminology, of the Eleusinian Mysteries.[14]

*No man can come to Me, except the Father which hath sent Me draw him* (John 6:44).

This verse is perverted by many Christians to excuse want of zeal in bringing the gospel to the unsaved, and by unbelievers to excuse their not coming to Christ. And this perversion of the Lord's words affords a colorable justification for saying that, if men do not accept the gospel, the fault lies with God, for He does not draw them.

But when read aright, the verse emphasizes a truth that permeates the whole Bible. Man's spiritual being is so utterly alienated from God that by the light of Nature he cannot even "see the kingdom of God," much less enter it. The records of the ministry do not contain a single case where a sinner who came to the Lord, confessing his blindness and helplessness, failed to receive light and blessing; but the Jews to whom these words were addressed spurned both Him and His teaching; and this

---

13. See note on Titus 3:5.
14. This subject is more fully treated in chapter 8 of the author's work, *The Bible or the Church*.

was His answer to their rejection of Him. The blind received their sight, and those who claimed to see were blinded. Dispensationally, these words were superseded by the Lord's further words in John 12:32. "For before the glorification of Christ the Father drew men to the Son, but now the Son Himself draws *all* to Himself."[15] But the principle underlying both statements is the same. For it is not in his moral, but in his spiritual nature, that man is utterly lost and dead. Saul the Pharisee was as moral as Paul the apostle. And have we not read of cases, even in heathendom, where without any light of revelation men have led a clean and upright life? And if this be possible for some, it is possible for all, and, therefore, God is just in punishing men for every breach of the moral law.

But did not the Lord say expressly that these Jews "had not had sin" if He "had not come and spoken unto them," and "had not done among them the works that none other did"? (John 15:22, 24). Yes, truly, but the sin there referred to was not their breaking the moral law, but their rejecting Christ and His testimony. For God holds none responsible for rejecting Christ save those who have heard of Christ.

All this throws light upon His words in John 6:44. They are not, as commonly supposed, a limitation placed upon the gospel; but they emphasize the solemnity both of preaching and hearing the gospel. By words and works that gave abundant proof of the presence and power of God, the Father had been drawing these proud religionists to Christ. But now their day of visitation was past, and they were left to their nature-darkness and incompetence to come to Him. And so is it in this present age when the Lord is drawing also unto Himself. True it is that but for divine "drawing" none would ever come. But sinners are not drawn heavenward in the sense in which criminals are drawn to prison. Whenever the gospel is preached in the power of the Holy Ghost sinners are being drawn to the Lord; but, alas! the many "resist the Holy Spirit."

---

15. Dean Alford, *Commentary*.

*He [the devil] was a murderer from the beginning* (John 8:44).

The Satan of "Christendom religion" is the mythical monster of Babylonian paganism.[16] And the general acceptance of this "Satan myth" has led to the popular misreading of these words. The vain boast of the Christ-rejecting Jews, that God was their Father, brought on them the scathing reply, "Ye are of your father the devil, and the desires of your father it is your will to do. He was a murderer from the beginning, and has not stood in the truth, because the truth is not in him. When he speaketh THE lie, he speaketh of his own, for he is a liar, and the father of IT (John 8:44)."

What mean these awful words, addressed by the Lord Jesus to earnest men of character and repute, who, under their responsibilities as religious leaders, deplored His teaching? "A murderer from the beginning." The beginning of what? Not of his own existence, for he was created in perfectness; nor yet of the Eden paradise, for long ere then Satan had dragged down others in his ruin. His being a murderer connects itself immediately with *the* truth which he refused, and *the* lie of which he is the father. These words of our Divine Lord give us, therefore, a glimpse into a past eternity, when, to the great intelligences of the heavenly world, God made known His purpose of a "first-born," who was "in all things to have the pre-eminence." The greatest of those heavenly beings claimed that place; and, rebelling against the divine purpose, he set himself from that hour to thwart its fulfilment.

And so during all the ages, as Luther wrote, "he hath no other business in hand but this only, to persecute and vex our Savior Christ." Therefore was it, that he compassed the ruin of our race. Therefore was it, that, in order to stamp out the house of David, he incited Athaliah to destroy "all the seed royal" (2 Kings 11), and at the Nativity he incited Herod to destroy "all the children that were in Bethlehem" (Matt. 2:16).

But it was not until the Temptation that his "lie" was plainly revealed. He there claimed to meet the Lord on more than equal terms. Having "led Him up," and given Him that myste-

---

16. This subject is more fully dealt with in the author's book, *The Silence of God* (Grand Rapids: Kregel Publications, 1978).

rious vision of earthly sovereignty, "the devil said unto Him, To Thee will I give this authority, and the glory of them, for it hath been delivered unto me, and to whomsoever I will I give it. If Thou, therefore, wilt worship before me, it shall all be Thine (Luke 4:6, 7)."

This was the bold assertion of his claim to be the true first-born, the rightful heir of creation, and therefore entitled to the worship of mankind. He is the awful being to whom Scripture accords the title of "the god of this world," not because the Supreme has delegated it, but because the world yields it to him.

As the temptation revealed him as the liar, Gethsemane and Calvary revealed him as the murderer. "Satan entered into Judas (Luke 22:3)," we read—a phrase that has no parallel in all the Scripture. And surely when the Evil One heard "Emmanuel's orphan-cry" upon the cross, and saw Christ's body carried to the tomb, he must have thought his victory was assured. But though foiled, he is still unconquered. For the Scriptures tell us of a supreme effort yet to come when—"woe to the hated race"—all the powers of hell will be at work to deceive mankind, and to thwart that coming triumph of the Lord of glory, "when He shall have put down all rule and all authority and power (1 Cor. 15:24)."

The devil of "Christendom religion" is a wonderful being who, like God Almighty, is omnipresent; for, the wide world over, he is by the side of every nursery cot, and at the elbow of every human being, making the babies naughty and the "grown-ups" vicious! This pestilent nonsense is believed even by spiritual Christians. Human nature being what it is, no devil is needed to make people tell lies, or to account for murders incited by the lusts and passions of evil men. But how can we account for the untold myriads of murders that have slandered the awful record of the professing "Christian church"—crimes more hideous than any that have been due to lust or greed? "Natural" murders (if such a phrase may be allowed) await the final judgment of the great day; but not these hell-born crimes of the so-called "Christian Church," "drunken with the blood of the saints and with the blood of the martyrs of Jesus."[17]

---

17. Revelation 17:6 and 19:2, and see Dean Alford's words quoted on p. 36, *ante.*

And yet these ghastly crimes were committed in the name of Christ, and by men who were outwardly devout and good; and they are justified, even today, by multitudes of people who are as kind-hearted and "religious" as the best of us! Yes, of a truth the devil has been a murderer from the beginning, and he is the *god* of this world.

May not the very many Psalms of David which contain references to conspiracies and plots against his life be read in the light of these words of the Lord Jesus about Satan? For surely there was no life in Old Testament story against which the devil's malice would have been more specially directed than that of David; for the devil must have known the prominence he held in the scheme of the Messianic purposes. In the opening sentence of the New Testament, Christ is designated "the son of David" (Matt. 1:1); and in the opening sentence of the Epistles, as " made of the seed of David according to the flesh (Rom. 1:3)." May we not give a new reading then to the so-called "imprecatory Psalms"? So far from expressing, as the Rationalists suppose, the cravings of an angry Kaiser for vengeance on his personal enemies, are they not the inspired utterances of the prophet-king with reference to his peculiar share in the conflict of the ages between Christ and His great enemy who was "a murderer from the beginning"?

*And whosoever liveth and believeth in Me shall never die* (John 11:26).

Here is the received exegesis of these words, as given by one of the best of our modern commentators:

"Faith in Me is the source of life, both here and hereafter, and those who have it, have Life, so that they shall never die," *physical death* being overlooked and disregarded, in comparison with that which is really and only death. . . There can hardly be any reference in verse 26 to the state of the living faithful at the Lord's coming (1 Cor. 15:51),—for although the apostle there, speaking of believers primarily and especially, uses the first person—the saying would be equally true of unbelievers, on whose bodies the change from the corruptible to the incorruptible will equally pass, and of whom the "shall never die" would here be equally true,— whereas the saying is one setting forth an exclusive privilege of the man that "liveth and believeth on Me."

This explains why our present verse is a "Misunderstood Text," for our theologians generally confound that coming of Christ, which is revealed as the present hope of His people, with the event of the last great *dies irae* in a very far-distant future. And thus, as in the case of certain other passages, a subtle argument is needed to vindicate the truth of the Lord's words. He called Lazarus from the tomb to die again; but "the living" of whom He here speaks are the "those who are alive and remain" of 1 Corinthians 15 (see p. 95, *post*); and they shall *never* die.

And here one may well ask, Who among us really believes that it is the same voice which recalled Lazarus from death that will yet call forth "all that are in their graves?" (John 5:28). Who among us believes that, even then, He could have spoken the word which would have summoned all the dead to life again? But though He had "all power," He ever held it in subjection to the will of His Father in heaven.

> *Every branch in Me that beareth not fruit He [the Father] taketh away* (John 15:2).

This passage is often perverted to undermine the great basic truth that we are saved by grace, and that our salvation is eternal. And the sixth verse is used to enforce this false reading. But the question here is not salvation, but fruit-bearing. The Lord's purpose in using this parable of the vine is not to cancel all His previous teaching about the eternal safety of the sinner who comes to Him, but to unfold truth of the highest practical importance for all who have been thus blessed. The language of the sixth verse, if carefully studied, will prevent our mistaking His meaning. "If any one does not abide in Me, he is cast out *as a branch*, and is withered." To bear fruit apart from Him is quite as impossible as to be saved apart from Him. The severed branch of another sort of tree might be used in some way. But as every Palestinian peasant knew, vine branches were useless; men gather them and cast them into the fire and they were burned. Indeed, these words of Christ about vine branches are, no doubt, a reference to Ezekiel 15:3, 4, "Shall wood be taken thereof to do any work? Behold, it is cast into the fire for fuel." They are not a doctrinal statement relating to the future destiny of men, but a parable to illustrate truth relating to the conduct and life of His people here and now.

> *Those that Thou gavest Me I have kept, and none of them is lost, but the son of perdition* (John 17:12).

This clearly implies that one of Christ's God-given ones may be finally lost. But the words the Lord actually used admit of a wholly different meaning. According to Bloomfield—and upon a question of Greek there is no higher authority—"*ei mê* is for *alla* when a negative sentence has preceded." And when words admit of different meanings, one of which is in accordance with, and the other in opposition to, other Scriptures, we must always accept the former. We cannot doubt, therefore, that in this passage the Lord used *ei mê* in the same sense as in Luke 4:25-27.

In the famine of Elijah's day there were many widows in Israel, but to none of them was the prophet sent; but (*ei mê*) he was sent to a *woman of Sidon*. There were many lepers in Israel in Elisha's day, but no one of them was cured; but (*ei mê*) *Naaman the Syrian* was cured. In these passages the *ei mê* does not introduce an exceptional case within the specified category, but a case belonging to a wholly different category. As Dean Plumptre puts it tersely, it is not an exception but a contrast (Ellicott's *New Testament Commentary*). To quote yet another instance, we read in Revelation 21:27, that there shall in no wise enter into the holy Jerusalem anything unclean, or he that maketh an abomination or a lie. But (*ei mê* —in marked contrast) they who are written in the Lamb's book of life shall enter there.

Now, let us read our present verse in this way, ignoring a punctuation which is arbitrary: "Those that Thou gavest me I have kept, and none of them is lost; but (*ei mê*) the son of perdition is lost, that the Scripture might be fulfilled." And when thus read, the Lord's words, instead of casting a doubt upon the truth that all His God-given ones are safe, becomes a signal confirmation of that truth.

To deal here with the awful mystery of Judas' ministry and

fall would be quite beyond the scope of these notes. But the Lord's mention of him indicates what, indeed, a careful study of the chapter would suggest, that in this portion of His prayer, down to the twenty-second verse, it is of His apostles the Lord is speaking. And if we overlook this, we lose a most precious insight into His mind and ways. These men have been His constant companions and fellow-workers during the ministry of His humiliation. But now He is leaving them in the world. And though the path on which He is entering leads to Gethsemane and Calvary, His thoughts and petitions are not about Himself, but altogether about them. Here is something, surely, to bring Him very near to us when, in any sphere of service, we are lonely or in peril.

# 3

# Misunderstood Texts
# in the Book of Acts

*The times of restitution of all things* (Acts 3:21).

The apostle Peter's second "Pentecostal sermon" has been dealt with on a preceding page.[1] No trained lawyer could frame words to teach more plainly that the "restitution of all things" will be the realization on earth, and in time, of Messianic Hebrew prophecy from Moses to Malachi. It might seem, therefore, that further notice of this verse would be unnecessary. But, thirty-eight years ago, an epoch-making book was written by an English clergyman to prove that the apostle's words point, not to earth and time, but to eternity and heaven. According to that writer, the teaching of this passage is that, at some unspecified era in the ages of ages, sinners who have gone to hell through rejecting the Atonement of Christ will pass to heaven as the result of working out atonement on their own account, by suffering punishment for their sins in hell. And this is now an article in the creed of multitudes of people.

But it will be asked, How is such an exegesis possible? The author's answer is, in effect: Because Scripture never really means what it seems to mean. Here are his words: "The letter of Scripture is a veil quite as much as a revelation, hiding while

---

1. See page 16 ff.

it reveals, and yet revealing what it hides, presenting to the eye something very different from that which is within." In other words, we may read into Holy Scripture any meaning which our fallacy makes us wish to find there.

But even assuming the truth of this writer's doctrine, can any person of ordinary intelligence suppose that the apostle would make it the gist and climax of his solemn appeal to the Christ-rejecting Jews? His aim is to bring them to repentance; and, *ex hypothesi*, he does this by assuring them that it is the teaching of "all the prophets, from Samuel and those that follow after, as many as have spoken," that even if they continue impenitent, they will reach heaven at last, though by a longer and harder road!

But, as every Bible student knows, whether this doctrine be true or false, it is entirely outside the scope of Hebrew prophecy. What concerns us here, however, is not its truth or falseness, but the meaning of Acts 3:21. And the question arises, whether the suggested exegesis of that verse does not justify the cynic's taunt, that in the sphere of religion there is nothing too wild to be believed.

*And [Stephen] said, Behold, I see the heavens opened, and the Son of Man standing on the right hand of God* (Acts 7:56)

These words are of exceptional interest and importance. "The Son of Man" is a Messianic title which is never used in Scripture save in relation to the Messianic Kingdom. And this is the only recorded instance in which the Lord was thus named by human lips. But that is not all. Mark the Lord's attitude, as seen by His martyred servant.

In Hebrews 10:11-13, the fact of His being *seated* is emphasized as of the highest doctrinal importance; but here He is seen *standing*. May we not read this in the light of the great Pentecostal proclamation of Acts 3:19, 20? The Lord is here seen in an attitude of expectancy. But the murder of Stephen was the crisis of the nation's destiny. The Lord's prayer upon the Cross had secured forgiveness for His own murderers. But the death of Stephen was, in effect, a repetition of that greatest of all human sins; and his murder was more definitely the act of the Jewish nation than even the crucifixion itself. Their Roman governors had no share in it. It was the result of a judicial decision on the part of the great council of the nation. The proto-martyr was thus the messenger sent after the king to say, "We will not have this man to reign over us." And the divine answer was to call out and commission the apostle of the Gentiles. And the Lord Jesus, till then "standing on the right hand of God," waiting to fulfil the Pentecostal promise, now "*sat down* on the right hand of God; from henceforth expecting till His enemies be made His footstool" (Heb. 10:12, 13).

*We [the Ephesian disciples] have not so much as heard whether there be any Holy Ghost* (Acts 19:2).

The translators of our English version showed extraordinary carelessness here. As Bengel writes, "[These disciples] could not have followed Moses or John the Baptist, without hearing of the Holy Spirit Himself."[2] The misunderstanding and error to which the passage has given rise are sufficiently met by the Revisers' translation of it: "Did ye receive the Holy Ghost when ye believed? And they said unto him, Nay, we did not so much as hear whether the Holy Ghost was given." To be strictly accurate, for "the Holy Spirit," we ought to read "Holy Spirit." *The* Holy Spirit was given to the church at Pentecost, but as and when we believe we receive the Holy Spirit.

*When the disciples came together to break bread* (Acts 20:7).

The record of the apostle Paul's visit to Troas is authoritatively interpreted as saying that, when he met with the disciples on the Sunday evening, he did not join them in eating the Lord's Supper; but when His address to them was interrupted by the Eutychus accident at midnight, he had "a private celebration of the Lord's Supper"! This strange whim of exegesis ignores the fact that "breaking bread" was a colloquial phrase in common use to mean "eating a meal." And while its few occurrences in Scripture will not warrant our either asserting or

---

2. John A. Bengel, *Bengel's New Testament Commentary*, (vol. 2), p. 876.

denying that the Lord's Supper was ever designated thus, there can be no reasonable doubt that when, as here, the words "had broken bread" are followed by "and had eaten," their meaning is that the apostle ate a meal. The gloss that the presence of the Greek article before bread is conclusive either way, is refuted by a reference to Luke 24:35.

The apostle's words in 1 Corinthians 11 indicate clearly that, among the abuses due to the practice of associating the Supper with the ordinary evening meal, was that some of the company shamed their poorer brethren by eating their own supper, and then leaving for home (vv. 21, 33). It is certain, therefore, that the Lord's Supper must have been the initial rite when they came together. And this being so, can there be any doubt respecting what took place at Troas? The apostle partook of the bread and juice with the assembled disciples; but afterwards, while the disciples were eating their evening meal, he continued talking with them till midnight; and not till then was he able to have a meal.

If the forty-second verse of Acts 2 stood alone, it would certainly favor the view that "the breaking of bread" there meant the Lord's Supper. But we must take account of the fact that the phrase recurs in verse 46, where the added words "did take their food with gladness" give proof that it had no sacred meaning. And surely it is improbable in the extreme that a colloquial phrase in common, vulgar use in everybody's mouth every day of the year would be chosen to designate such a solemn and holy rite.

In the East the phrase is still in daily use, for "bread" is a generic term for food. "When the dinner is ordered, it is still, as of old, by the modest words, 'Set on bread,' no matter how elaborate the feast; and some Oriental dinners consist of more than twenty courses."[3] Thus it was that Joseph ordered the banquet to be served for his brothers (Gen. 43:31). "And in the East, bread is never cut, for it is thought absolutely wicked to put a knife in it."[4]

---

3. James Neil, *Everyday Life in the Holy Land*, p. 193.
4. *Ibid.*, p. 82.

# 4

## Misunderstood Texts in the Epistles of Paul

*They that are in the flesh cannot please God* (Romans 8:8).

This verse is used to support the dogma that, because of the Fall, man's nature is so utterly depraved that he is incapable of leading a moral and upright life. As the Westminster divines express it, "We are utterly indisposed, disabled, and made opposite to all good."

This theology obviously refutes the righteousness of God in punishing men for their sins. In fact, it represents Him as a tyrant who punishes the lame for limping and the blind for losing their way. No less obviously does it clash with plain and patent facts. For the outward life of Saul the Pharisee was as pure and upright as that of Paul the apostle. And in our own day we ourselves have known many unbelievers whose conduct and character would bear comparison with those of many a Christian.

It is not in the moral sphere of his being, but in the *spiritual*, that man is hopelessly depraved and lost. Therefore was it that the "zeal of God" of the Jewish leaders led them to crucify the Christ of God, and that Gamaliel's great disciple, though a pattern moralist, became a persecutor and blasphemer. And the seventh verse must not be read to mean that men were not subject to the letter of the law of Sinai. In calling that code "the moral law," theology means that it is the law of our being. And thus regarded, the Pharisees were scrupulous in their obedience to it. But "the carnal mind" is absolutely incapable of appreciating its *spiritual* significance. The difference between the blind and those who have their sight is not that they see less clearly, but that they do not see at all. And quite as absolute is the antithesis between the carnal and the spiritual. But just as a blind man may have full use of his other physical faculties, so the carnal man may be a thorough moralist. It is no answer to say that this is true only of some; for the fact that it is true of any is proof that God is righteous in judging *all*.

Let no one dismiss all this as though it were of merely academic interest. There are few errors more harmful in the present day. For such a false reading of Scripture disparages it in the judgment of thoughtful men, and fosters the new enlightenment which has so degraded Germany, and which is rapidly leavening the British churches of the Reformation. And no less evil is its influence upon spiritual Christians. For in spite of the solemn, divine warning that Satan fashions himself as an angel of light, and his ministers as ministers of righteousness, Christians are thus betrayed into recognizing as ministers of Christ any man who commends himself as a minister of righteousness. And the result is that "truth is fallen in the street," and certain of our divinity schools and theological colleges are supplying our pulpits with agnostics and rationalists.

*Whom He did foreknow, He also did predestinate to be conformed to the image of His Son* (Romans 8:29).

The word *proorizo*, on which theology has reared such an imposing edifice, occurs only in the four following passages: Acts 4:28; Romans 8:29, 30; 1 Corinthians 11:7; and Ephesians 1:5, 11. In only two of these, moreover, is it used with reference to the destiny of men; and never in relation to *life*, but only to special positions of blessing to which the redeemed are predestinated. In our present verse it is "to be conformed to the image of His Son." And in keeping with this, in Ephesians 1:5 we are said to be predestinated "unto adoption as sons," and in verse 11 it is "to be His heritage" (R.V.). The word in the fifth verse is not "children," but *sons*; and in Scripture "son" is not a mere synonym for offspring, but betokens special dignity and privilege. Whether these statements are true of all the saved we may not dogmatize, but here they refer to the redeemed of this Christian dispensation.

The words, "whom He did foreknow," must not be ignored. But it would be foreign to the purpose of these notes to enter here upon the controversy with which they are associated. The practice of throwing positive statements of Scripture into an alternative negative form, and then basing doctrines upon inferences deduced from them as thus presented, is a fruitful cause of grievous error. By this treatment, for instance, the words of our present verse, which are given to promote the comfort and confidence of the Christian, are so perverted as to become a limitation upon the gospel of the grace of God.

> *I could wish that myself were accursed from Christ for my brethren, my kinsmen according to the flesh* (Romans 9:3).

The "difficulty" of this verse would not seem so perplexing if it were translated more correctly. Dean Alford's note is, "*I was wishing*—this imperfect tense . . . implies, as very often, a half expression of a desire." Or, as Bishop Ellicott's *New Testament Commentary* puts it, "*I could have wished*. The wish, of course, relates to what was really impossible." And this is the view of numerous authorities who take the word *anathema* to mean "cut off from Christ for ever in eternal perdition."

But as Greek scholars allow a wide range of meaning to the word, the question is legitimate whether it be in harmony with the tone and tenor of Scripture to suppose that the Holy Spirit would inspire any one to frame and utter such a statement. Or, entirely eliminating the element of inspiration, whether such an outburst of unrestrained feeling be consistent with the known character of the Apostle Paul. Is not such a reading of the passage calculated to lower our estimate of him *as a man*? Let us inquire then in what sense he elsewhere used the word *anathema*.

Now we know that the gospel of grace was his special "trust." And so strong was his feeling on this subject that in warning the Galatian church against any one, whether man or angel, who preached any gospel other than he himself had preached, that twice he used the words, "Let him be anathema" (1:8, 9). Having regard then to his treatment of this subject in Philippians 1:15-18, is it credible that he meant, "Let him be damned for eternity"? If I do not appeal also to his use of the word in 1 Corinthians 16:23, it is because the Galatian reference seems conclusive. In 1 Corinthians 12:2, the only other occurrence of the word in his epistles, it is evidently used as the technical term for excommunication among the Jews.

It is very noteworthy that our verse is usually considered without reference to the teaching of the epistle in which it occurs, or even to the immediate context. But, as Bloomfield remarks, between the eighth chapter and the ninth "there is a closer connection than commentators have been aware." And he might have added that, between chapter 9 and the two following chapters, this connection is closer still. The inquiry this suggests is as interesting as it is important. The received exegesis is a legacy from days when the prophecies and promises relating to Israel's future were "spiritualized" to make them refer to "the Christian church"; and it was tacitly assumed that nothing remained for Israel but judgment and wrath. And this seemed to account for such a strange outburst of passionate feeling on the part of the apostle. But these chapters show us that, even as he penned these words, he had prominently in view, first that Israel's rejection was but temporary, and secondly that during this age of grace "there is no difference between the Jew and the Gentile," and therefore the individual Israelite is in no respect at a disadvantage; for salvation is equally free to all (10:12, 13).

Moreover, at the time when he was writing, the Jewish converts everywhere, and notably in Rome, far outnumbered the Gentiles. Are we to conclude then that the burden of his impassioned longing was that a still larger proportion of Jews might be brought in? A most legitimate longing surely, but to express it in such terms would be unworthy, I will not say of an inspired apostle, but of any sensible man with a well-balanced mind. And this very chapter vetoes the suggestion that what he had in view was the salvation of every Israelite—"all the seed of Abraham according to the flesh (Rom. 9:3)."

What, then, can have been his meaning? As it was neither

that *some* Israelites might be saved, nor that *more* Israelites might be saved, nor yet that *all* Israelites might be saved, there is only one conclusion open to us, namely, that the burden upon his heart was the condition of Israel *nationally*, and that he longed intensely for their restoration to the position they had lost. For the privileges and blessings specified in the fourth and fifth verses of this chapter did not pertain to the individual Hebrew, but to the nation. And his argument, broken, *more suo*, by many a parenthesis, reaches a climax with the words, "And so all Israel shall be saved" (11:26) —that is, Israel as a nation. And the longing of his heart was to witness that consummation.

But, it will be asked, would the apostle Paul have bartered his eternal destiny for the realization of such a hope as that? I would answer (*contra mundum*, if needs be) that no possible consideration would have betrayed him into uttering, or even harboring, such a wish. And this emboldens me to suggest a new reading of the passage. We know from his writings with what holy pride Paul regarded his high office as the apostle of the Lord, and his portion in the Body of Christ, with the heavenly calling and glory pertaining to it. And yet so burdened was he by "great heaviness and continual sorrow" in his heart, on account of the condition of his nation, that for their sake he could wish to be cut off from Christ in respect of all this dispensational position of transcendental privilege and glory, and to take the lower place of blessing in the earthly kingdom, with his "kinsmen according to the flesh," if by such a sacrifice he could win their restoration to favor, forthwith, as the covenant people of God.

And this reading of the third verse brings it into harmony with the chapter as a whole, the burden of which is, not the spiritual salvation of individual sinners, but racial and dispensational privilege and blessing.

*Jacob have I loved, but Esau have I hated* (Romans 9:13).

As noticed by certain expositors, the burden of this chapter, as a whole, is racial and dispensational privilege and blessing. And this applies very specially to this thirteenth verse. For it plainly appears by referring to the opening words of Malachi, from which it is quoted, that the Esau here intended is not the individual, but the Edom family or race. And if we are to infer from the eighth verse that all Esau's descendants are "children of wrath," we must infer also, in direct opposition to the apostle's argument, that all Isaac's posterity are children of God. The story of Esau might well have checked the dogmatism of the predestination controversy. For "the purpose of God according to election" was not that Jacob should be eternally saved, and Esau lost, but that the elder should serve the younger. And Genesis 25 plainly indicates the sin which led to this stern decree. "Esau despised his birthright," and as this position of influence and blessing was divinely bestowed, his sin in bartering it for a mess of pottage is branded as "profanity," and a place of repentance was denied him. It was not a question of his eternal destiny, but of his forfeited birthright. And what concerns us is to profit by the warning of Hebrews 12:15-17, and also to shun the profane inquiry whether his sin was not due to "the purpose of God according to election."

A reference to our Lord's teaching in Luke 14:26 will save us from reading this verse in a false light because of the meaning of our English word "hate." The Greek word is here used as "equivalent to *loving less,* a qualified sense, of which there are many examples both in the Septuagint and the New Testament" (Bloomfield, vol. 1, p. 36), and as the *Speaker's Commentary* well says, "The exaggerated sense of positive hate is quite forbidden by the record of the ample blessing bestowed on Esau."

*The Scripture saith unto Pharaoh, Even for this same purpose have I raised thee up, that I might show My power in thee* (Romans 9:17).

Does this mean that God called Pharaoh into existence for the purpose of making known His divine power in destroying him? Such a profane reading of the verse has no scriptural warrant. The word here used does not mean "to call into being" but to "rouse," or "wake up." The marginal reading of Exodus 9: 16 is the right one, "For this cause have I *made thee stand,* to show in thee My power." And in the Greek version this is rendered, "For this purpose hast thou been preserved until now."

The divine command he treated with contempt, "Who is the Lord that I should obey His voice?" (Exod. 5:2), was his impious rejoinder. And when the spoken word was accredited by miraculous power, he called upon his demon-possessed magicians to parody the miracles. It would have been in the spirit of that dispensation if God had struck him down in his sin. But he was preserved—he was made to stand—as a foil for the display of the power of God, and that the name of God "might be declared throughout all the earth."

And the twenty-first verse of Romans 9 must not be read apart from the twenty-second, but as exemplifying the main teaching of the chapter. The contrast it expresses is not between life and death, but between honor and dishonor. With the same clay the potter may form one vessel for use on the table of a king, while he designs another for some base, though equally useful, purpose. But a potter who would make a vessel with the deliberate purpose of destroying it must be a maniac of a dangerous type. And the twenty-second verse puts to shame the profane thought that God is here compared to a maniac potter!

Mark the words, "What if God, purposing to shew forth His wrath and to make His power known, *endured with much long-suffering* the vessels of wrath fitted to destruction?" In view of these words no one may dare to assert that Pharaoh might not have found mercy had he cast himself upon God in repentance and confession. His case was akin to that of the Christ-rejecting Jews in the days of His ministry. It was because they refused the light that God blinded their eyes. And if God hardened Pharaoh's heart, it was because he himself had closed it against abundant proofs of the divine presence and power. Both cases exemplify a principle that governs "the ways of God to men." Toward them that fear Him, His mercy is boundless, but we do well to remember the solemn warning of Psalm 18:26, "With the perverse Thou wilt shew Thyself froward." No one may despise God with impunity.

*My gospel* (Romans 16:25, 26).

Strange it seems that expositors should have failed to notice the clearly marked difference between the gospel of the opening verses of Romans and that of the apostle's postscript at its close. We read the epistle amiss if we fail to notice what an important place its teaching accords to the Hebrew Christians, who doubtless were the majority in the local church. For in early days it was "to Jews only" that the gospel was preached; and the word which had won them was "the gospel of God, which He promised afore by His prophets in the Holy Scriptures concerning His Son who was *born of the seed of David*" (1:2, 3, R.V.). This was the hope of every true Israelite. In keeping with it were the apostle's words to the "chief of the Jews" in Rome: "For the hope of Israel I am bound with this chain." And his answer to the charge on which he was imprisoned was that his preaching to the Jews was based entirely on their own Scriptures (Acts 26:22).

But the gospel which he preached to Gentiles he had received by special revelation to himself; and to communicate that gospel to his brother apostles was the purpose of his third visit to Jerusalem (Gal. 2:2). In writing to Timothy he spoke of it as "committed to *my trust.*" And this is the "my gospel" of Romans 2:16 and of our present verse. Here are his words: "Now to Him that is able to stablish you according to my gospel, even the preaching of Jesus Christ, according to the revelation of a mystery which was kept secret since the world began, but now is made manifest, and by prophetic writings, according to the commandment of the everlasting God, made known to all the nations unto obedience of faith."

I have rendered the first *kai* in this sentence by "even," for it is certain that the apostle did not mean to distinguish between the gospel of Christ and a gospel of his own! And "the Scriptures of the prophets" is a mistranslation which reduces his words to an absurdity, for he is thus made to say that this "mystery" gospel was kept secret in all the past, and yet that it was taught in Old Testament Scriptures. His actual words are "prophetic writings," i.e. the inspired Epistles of the New Testament. For a prophet is "one who, moved by the Spirit of God, declares what he has received by inspiration" (*Grimm's Lexicon*); and therefore "prophetic writings" is equivalent to *inspired* writings, the element of foretelling the future being purely incidental.

And there can be no doubt that the "mystery" of our verse is what the apostle calls elsewhere "the mystery of the gospel"— the reign of grace, which is the great basic truth of the distinctly Christian revelation—a truth which was not, and obviously could not be, declared until the covenant people were set aside. For grace is as incompatible with *covenant*, or special favor of any kind, as it is with works.

The twenty-fifth verse is sometimes read with an emphasis on the definite article before the word "mystery," the purpose being to suggest a reference to the truth of the church the Body of Christ. But this is an obvious error, not only because there is no article in the Greek, but because the "mystery" of the Body is a truth for the Christian, whereas here the apostle's subject is the gospel which was to be "made known to all the Gentiles" (R. V. margin).

*Who [Christ] of God is made unto us wisdom, and righteousness, and sanctification, and redemption* (1 Corinthians 1:30).

The wonderful truth of this passage is obscured by faulty translation, largely due, no doubt, to neglect of the typology of Scripture. The blood of the Passover, sprinkled upon the dwellings of the Israelites, brought them deliverance from the death judgment passed upon Egypt. But it gave them neither right nor fitness to come near to God; and when His glory was displayed on Sinai they were sternly warned not to approach the mountain (Exod. 19:21). None but Moses, "the mediator of the covenant," could be allowed to enter the divine presence. Not until the blood of the covenant had been shed and sprinkled upon them, could even the elders of Israel come near to God (Exod. 24). And they then went up as the representatives of the people.

And forthwith there followed the command, "Let them make me a tabernacle that I may dwell among them" (Exod. 25:8).

The demands of divine righteousness had been satisfied before their deliverance from Egypt. But God is holy as well as righteous; and it was not until they had been sanctified by the blood of the covenant, as they had already been justified by the blood of the Passover, that their redemption was complete.

In the light of these types we can grasp the meaning of the apostle's words. All that these sacrifices typified, Christ is made to us in fulness of fact and truth. He is "made unto us wisdom, and both righteousness and sanctification, even redemption"— redemption in its fulness as including all we need, not only to secure relief from wrath, but to bring us into covenant relationship with God, and to give us access to His presence.

For redemption is not a blessing added to justification and sanctification, as our English versions would suggest. It is an inclusive term, as appears plainly from the apostle's words. But both A.V. and R.V. ignore the *te kai* in the verse, which ought, of course, to be rendered "both," as in verse 24.[1] And no less, of course, the second *kai* should be translated "even." When rightly rendered, therefore, the passage reads: "Who of God is made unto us wisdom, and both righteousness and sanctification, even redemption." Sanctification, like justification, has a twofold aspect, the one complete in Christ, and the other to be realized in the Christian life.

> *I determined not to know anything among you, save Jesus Christ, and Him crucified* (1 Corinthians 2:2).

"We have here a statement of what was the subject matter of apostolic teaching." This sentence, quoted from a standard commentary, would be most apt if it referred to the apostle's words, "We preach Christ Jesus the Lord" (2 Cor. 4: 5). But it is strange that any one could have penned it here, after studying the epistle as a whole, or chapter 15 in particular. Indeed, the opening verses of chapter 3 refute such a misreading of the apostle's language.

Ignoring the emphasis which rests upon the words "among

---

1. In their marginal note the Revisers give us the "both," but they make it both of three!

you," the verse is thus used, not only to condone, but to commend, any system of Bible teaching which is limited to "the simple gospel." But the apostle is not here describing the subject matter of his general teaching, but the scope and character of his preaching when he brought the gospel to Corinth. The Greek was a wisdom-worshiper; and such a man as Paul might have so preached that he would have had all Corinth at his feet. "The many" did thus "huckster the Word of God" (2 Cor. 2:17); but as for the Apostle, neither his speech (*logos*) nor his preaching (i.e., neither the matter nor the manner of it) was in persuasive words of (human) wisdom (1 Cor. 2:4).

"Flesh and blood hath not revealed it unto thee, but My Father who is in heaven (Matt. 16:17)," was the Lord's response to Peter's confession of His deity; and if this was true of the apostle, even after he had witnessed all the amazing miracles of the Ministry, how intensely true it must be of other men! And so here, the aim of the apostle Paul was that the faith of the converts should stand in divine power, and not in human wisdom. In their case, moreover, such special care was needed that, even after their conversion, he felt restrained in unfolding to them "the deep things of God" (1 Cor. 2:10; see 3:1, 2).

"We do speak wisdom among the perfect," he says in this very chapter (v. 6). The word here rendered "the perfect" is translated "men" in 14:20, and "of full age" in Hebrews 5:14. But spiritually the Corinthians were not men, nor of full age, but mere babes; and so he had to treat them as babes and to feed them with milk.

As he had already said, "Christ is the wisdom of God" (1:24). Still fuller his words in Colossians 2:2, 3 —"that they may know the mystery of God, even Christ, in whom are all the treasures of wisdom and knowledge hidden." Therefore the phrase "to know nothing but Christ" might in a real sense describe the apostle's ministry. But the main emphasis of our present text rests on the closing words, "*even Him crucified.*" The words of 1:22-24 explain the apostle's meaning, "Seeing that Jews ask for signs, and Greeks seek after wisdom, we [in antithesis to all this] preach Christ crucified, unto Jews an offence, and unto Greeks foolishness; but unto them who are the called [i.e. to Christians] we preach Christ the power of God and the wisdom of God."

*Know ye not that the unrighteous shall not inherit the kingdom of God?* (1 Corinthians 6:9).

Exclusion from "the millennial kingdom" we are told by some, will be the penalty imposed on Christians who lapse into immoral practices. And in proof of this we are referred to such passages as 1 Corinthians 6:9, 10; Galatians 5:21; Ephesians 5:5; etc. This assumes that "the kingdom of God" is a synonym for the millennial kingdom, an error which is exposed by the very first passage in which the phrase occurs in the Epistles. In Romans 14:17, we read: "The kingdom of God is not meat and drink, but righteousness and peace and joy in the Holy Ghost." This reminds us of the Lord's words to Nicodemus. The world and its religion is the natural sphere, but the kingdom of God is spiritual; and none can enter it, none can see it, without a new birth by the Spirit. This is a truth of present and universal application. 1 Corinthians 15:50, which refers to the future, is a still more decisive refutation of the error. There we read that "flesh and blood cannot inherit the kingdom of God"; that is, can have no place or part in it. But, as we all know, "flesh and blood"—men in their natural bodies—will be in the millennial kingdom, or, to use the scriptural phrase, the kingdom of heaven (see pp. 11-14, *ante*). Then again we recall the exhortation of 1 Thessalonians 2:12, "that ye would walk worthy of God, who hath called you unto His kingdom and glory." This is explained by 2 Thessalonians 1:5, "that ye may be counted worthy of the kingdom of God"—a reference not to the future state, but to the place and calling of the Christian here and now. It is akin to the exhortations of Ephesians 4:1 (R.V.), "I beseech you to walk worthily of the calling wherewith ye were called." For it is a present truth, and a fact of practical import, that the Christian has been "translated into the kingdom of the Son of His love" (Col. 1:13). As a matter of fact, it is more than doubtful whether the millennial kingdom is ever referred to in the epistles of the apostle Paul.

This scheme of exegesis, moreover, would teach us to acknowledge an "evil liver" as a Christian. But as 2 Timothy 2:19 tells us, the divine seal has two faces: "The Lord knoweth them that are His" is the Godward side of it; the other, which is to govern *our* action, is "Let every one that nameth the name of Christ depart from iniquity." But, we are told, the "incestuous person" in Corinth was a Christian. The inspired apostle so decided; but to us it is not given to read the Godward face of the divine seal, and we are bound to judge others by their profession and conduct. To acknowledge as a Christian any one who is living in open sin is to be false to the Lord. But if every penitent has a claim upon Christian sympathy, surely one whom we have regarded as a fellow believer ought to be treated with unbounded patience and pity and Christian love. And let us not forget that there are sins more heinous than immoral acts. Some of the "unfortunates" of the streets may be nearer the kingdom than are men of high repute in the professing church, who deny the deity of the Lord Jesus Christ, or scoff His authority as a teacher (Matt. 21:31). To acknowledge such men in any way is to become "partaker of their evil deeds" (2 John 10, 11). The doom of Sodom will be more tolerable than that of devout Capernaum (Matt. 11:23, 24).

*Lest . . . when I have preached to others, I myself should be a castaway* (1 Corinthians 9:27).

Were it not for a morbid tendency to seize upon any Scripture which can be perverted to undermine the truth of grace, no one could find a difficulty here. For the subject, not only of the immediate context, but of the whole chapter, is the apostle's *ministry*, and has no sort of reference to salvation. As he says in the twenty-fourth verse, in a race *all* run, but *one* receives the prize. But if it was found that the winner, even though he had proclaimed the rules of the contest to the others, had himself violated these rules, he was refused the prize—he was "rejected" (*adokimos*).

The suggestion that the apostle Paul was in doubt whether he might not himself be finally lost is quite unworthy of consideration. His epistles one and all refute it. The word *adokimos* was originally applied to base coin, and this affords a clue to its meaning here. A genuine coin never becomes base, and an *adokimos* coin is base *ab initio*. Hence Bloomfield's reading of 2 Corinthians 13:5, "Unless indeed ye be not genuine Christians." And in our present verse the word is explained by Bengel to mean "unworthy of a prize or crown, as in the public games."

A morbid readiness to undermine the truth of grace leads to a like perversion of the apostle's words, "I have kept the faith," in 2 Timothy 4:7, as though they meant, "I have kept on believing in Christ." But here again he is speaking of his ministry. For the *gar* of verse 6 directly connects his words about himself with his charge to Timothy in verse 5. And what he says is not "I have maintained *my* faith," but "I have safeguarded *the faith*," a term that is defined to mean generally "the sum of Christian doctrines." In Paul's case it meant specially, no doubt, the great truth of the gospel of grace which was his peculiar trust. "That which [God] hath committed unto me," he calls it—that "good deposit" which was in turn entrusted to Timothy.[2]

> *What shall they do who are baptized for the dead?*
> (1 Corinthians 15:29).

Bengel remarks that the variety of interpretations of this passage is so great that even a catalog of them "would require a dissertation." And he goes on to say that the practice to which the apostle is supposed to refer "came into use from a wrong interpretation of this very passage."

Even were it otherwise, and heretical sects had already adopted pagan practices of this kind, the idea is utterly absurd that the apostle Paul would have appealed to them as a climax to his sublime argument for the Resurrection; and to attribute such a triviality to the inspiring Spirit of God would be profane.

The following solution of this very difficult passage has been offered by the late Dr. E. W. Bullinger. As in the ancient texts, there is no punctuation, save the greater pauses, he discards the received punctuation of the verse. He notices that in Scripture the word *nekros* with the article usually denotes dead bodies, corpses; whereas without the article it denotes dead *people*, persons who are dead. And he proceeds to use the passage as a

---

2. Such is the right of 2 Timothy 1:12, 14, as indicated by the American Revisers in their marginal note. See also note on Romans 16:25, p. 76, *ante*.

typical illustration of the figure of speech known as *ellipsis*. And construing the passage thus, he renders it, "What shall they do that are being baptized? It is for the dead [for corpses] if the dead [dead people] rise not."[3] To make this fully intelligible we must take note of the meaning of the apostle's words, "What shall they do?" They are equivalent to "What will become of them?" (Dean Alford). For the Greek word *poieô* has a range of meaning nearly as wide as the Hebrew *âsâh*, which it represents in the Greek version of such passages as Jeremiah 5:31 and 12:5; which might be rendered, "What will become of you at last!" and "What will become of you in the swelling of Jordan!" These are not inquiries, but warning exclamations. And so here. The apostle is not propounding a thesis for discussion. His purpose is to put an end to discussion in the whole matter; so he exclaims, "If the dead rise not, what is to become of people who are being baptized!"[4]

The apostle's argument, therefore, may be stated as follows: Baptism symbolizes death with Christ; what meaning has it then, if there be no resurrection? For if Christ was not raised, our oneness with Him in death points only to the tomb. In a word, his appeal is not to a despicable pagan heresy, but to the teaching of a great Christian ordinance.

"Thus the expression 'baptized for the dead' vanishes from the Scriptures; and it is banished from theology, for the assumed practice is gathered only from this passage, and is unknown to history apart from it."[5]

*Behold, I show you a mystery; we shall not all sleep, but we shall all be changed . . .* (1 Corinthians 15:51 ff.).

As this passage is generally supposed to refer to "the Second Advent," it claims prominent notice in any list of misunderstood texts. For, both in standard theology and in the popular use of the phrase, "the Second Advent" is the last great coming of

---

3. E. W. Bullinger, *How to Enjoy the Bible* (Grand Rapids: Kregel Publications, 1990), p. 53.
4. This is the force of the present participle.
5. E. W. Bullinger, *Figures of Speech Used in the Bible* (Grand Rapids: Baker Book House).

Christ in an indefinitely remote future, whereas the coming
here revealed is the present hope of the Christian. The one,
moreover, is His coming to execute judgment upon the world;
the other is His coming to call His chosen people to their heavenly home.

But this is not all. Mark the apostle's words, "I show you a
*mystery*"; and in the Epistles the word "mystery" indicates some
truth which had remained secret up to the time of the apostles.[6]
Seeing then that the Lord's coming in judgment was prophe-
sied by "Enoch, the seventh from Adam" (Jude 14, 15), it cannot be the "mystery" of 1 Corinthians 15. Neither can His coming
as the Son of Man, for that also is an Old Testament truth; and
it had prominence in the Lord's own ministry. Indeed, these
several "comings" have practically nothing in common, save
that they all relate to Christ.

To understand this subject aright, we must keep in view the
distinctive character of the special Christian revelation which
followed the setting aside of the covenant people. And the
"mystery" truths of that revelation are inseparably allied. Its
basic truth is grace enthroned. And grace vastly transcends
mercy, and it is inconsistent with covenant. It was in pure grace
that God gave the covenant to Abraham; but when a covenant
or promise has been granted, it is to His *faithfulness* we trust for
the fulfilment of it. And the covenant with Abraham has not
been cancelled, although it is in waiting during this present
dispensation. This is another of the mysteries of the Christian
revelation (Rom. 11:25). It is not that the covenant people are in
subjection to Gentile supremacy: that dates back to the days of
Nebuchadnezzar. Neither is it that they are under divine displeasure because of their impenitence: that is no new thing in
Israel's history. The "mystery" is that they are temporarily rele-
gated in all respects to the position of the Gentiles among whom
they are scattered. In other words, their condition during this
Christian age is precisely what it would be if the Abrahamic
covenant had never been granted.

And this abnormal condition of things gives rise to questions
that are nowhere dealt with in Old Testament Scriptures. What,

---

6. See p. 13, *ante.*

for instance, is to be the status, so to speak, of the saved of this dispensation? To that question the mystery of the church, the Body of Christ, supplies the answer. But, as already noticed, Romans 11 teaches explicitly that the present dispensation is parenthetical and transient: how then is it to be brought to an end? Now in the same sense in which we aver that God cannot lie, we may aver that He cannot act upon incompatible principles at the same time. Therefore, so long as the proclamation is in force that "there is no difference between the Jew and the Gentile," God cannot make a difference by giving the Jew a position of peculiar privilege and favor. It follows, therefore, that the present dispensation cannot merge gradually in the dispensation which is to follow it. The change must be marked by a crisis. And here the teaching of Scripture is clear and definite. The nature of the crisis is revealed in 1 Corinthians 15, and in other passages in the Epistles. It will be that coming of Christ which Bengel designates "the hope of the church." But, as he truly says, "The churches have forgotten the hope of the Church."

Plain speaking is necessary here. In common with the other "mystery" truths of the distinctive Christian revelation, this truth of the Lord's coming was lost in the early church, prior to the era of the Patristic theologians. So entirely was it lost, indeed, that in this Corinthian passage several of the most ancient manuscripts read, "We shall all sleep, but we shall not all be changed"—a corruption apparently designed to reconcile the apostle's words with the "Second Advent" doctrine which had been already formulated. Would that those gifted and holy men had left far fuller personal records and fewer theological writings. Their life story would have stimulated faith during all the centuries, and the Reformers would have studied the Bible with minds unbiased by their doctrinal teaching. And we in our day would not be so often embarrassed by having to make choice between the teaching of theology and of the New Testament.

As the misunderstanding of this Scripture is due in great measure to the fact that the truth it teaches has been forgotten, it may be well to notice here a few kindred passages in other epistles. First Corinthians was written at a comparatively early period in the apostle's ministry; and it is suggested by unbelievers that in later years he discovered his mistake in supposing that the coming of the Lord should be deemed a present hope. By very many Christians, moreover, this view is in a vague way accepted, although they hesitate to give expression to it.

What, then, are the facts? The epistle to the Philippians was written from his Roman prison at a time when his active ministry seemed to be at an end. And in these circumstances it was that he wrote the words, "Our citizenship is in heaven; from whence also we wait for a Savior, the Lord Jesus Christ: who shall fashion anew the body of our humiliation, that it may be conformed to the body of His glory" (Phil. 3:20, 21). Now the word here rendered "wait" is the strongest that any language could supply to express the earnest expectation of something believed to be imminent. According to Bloomfield, "it signifies properly to thrust forward the head and neck as in anxious expectation of hearing or seeing something." An illustration of its meaning might be found in the pathetic story of the mother of Sisera's vigil for her son's return, "Through the window she looked forth, and cried through the lattice, Why is his chariot so long in coming? Why tarry the wheels of his chariots?" (Judg. 5:28).

Such, then, is the divinely chosen word, to indicate what ought to be our attitude toward the return of Christ. And it is a kindred word that the apostle uses in his epistle to Titus, dated probably in the very year of his martyrdom, where he tells us that the training of the school of grace leads us to live "looking for that blessed hope" (Tit. 2:12, 13). As Dean Alford says: "The apostolic age maintained that which ought to be the attitude of all ages, constant expectation of the Lord's return."

Very special weight attaches to these *dicta* of Bloomfield and Alford, just because neither of them was an exponent of the truth of "the blessed hope." But upon any question respecting the meaning and use of a Greek word there is no higher authority than Bloomfield. And as a commentator, Alford is specially noted for fairness and British common sense. Every honest-minded student of the Epistles, moreover, will endorse the conclusion that, to the very end of his ministry, the apostle inculcated— not belief in the doctrine of the Second Advent, but —"constant expectation of," and eager waiting and watching for, the Lord's return.

Certain it is, therefore, that if the coming of Christ, of which these epistles speak, be the same as the coming of the Son of Man of Matthew 24, the apostle's words are in flat and flagrant opposition to the Lord's explicit teaching. For His warning was clear and emphatic that "the coming of the Son of Man" must not be looked for until after the coming of Antichrist, the horrors of the great tribulation, and the awful signs and portents foretold in Messianic prophecy. If then these several Scriptures relate to the same event, we must jettison either Matthew 24 or the Pauline Epistles. For the attempt to reconcile them indicates hopeless mental obtuseness. And these results will be confirmed by a study of the Thessalonian Epistles (see pp. 106 and 110, *post*).

## *The letter killeth* (2 Corinthians 3:6).

This text is freely used to discredit Scripture. Here is the verse *in extenso*: "Who [God] also hath made us able ministers of the New Testament; not of the letter, but of the spirit; for the letter killeth, but the spirit giveth life." And the commonly received exegesis of this is that the apostle was made a minister, not of the letter (i.e., the words), but of the spirit, of the gospel; for the letter of the gospel kills. Many a page might be filled with extracts from the apostle's own writings to prove the utter falseness of this. But the following utterance from the lips of the Lord Himself may suffice: "The *words* that I speak unto you are spirit and are life" (John 6:63).

Verse 7 clearly indicates that the contrast intended by the apostle's words is not at all between the letter and the spirit of the gospel, but between the ministration of death in the law— "in *letters* engraven on stones" (R.V. margin), and the ministration of life—or, as verse 8 expresses it, "the ministration *of the spirit*"—in the gospel. And he emphasizes the fact that God had called him to the higher ministry of the life-giving gospel, and not of the death-dealing law. Now by the figure of metonymy, so familiar to every Bible student, he seizes on the key-words "letter" and "spirit" to represent law and gospel, respectively.

> *We must all appear before the judgment seat of Christ*
> (2 Corinthians 5:10).

To understand these words aright, we must study the context. And the chapter should be read in the Revised Version, for, owing probably to the far-reaching influence of Chrysostom's brilliant homily upon it, our Authorized Version is marred by mistranslation in some important respects.

The symbolism of the preceding verses is graphic and yet simple. Our "natural body" is likened to the tabernacle, the "spiritual body" to a building —not, like the temple, built on earth by human hands, but a building of God, eternal, and in the heavens. Then the symbolism changes. Death is likened to our being unclothed, "found naked"; and our receiving our heavenly body without passing through death is symbolized by our being "clothed upon"—the change which the coming of the Lord will bring to those "who are alive and remain" when mortality shall be swallowed up of life. And our longing is for this (v. 2). Not that death has terrors; for "being always of good courage," we are "willing rather to be absent from the body, and to be at home with the Lord" (2 Cor. 5:8).

Then come the words (perverted in our A.V.), "Wherefore also we make it our aim [literally, we are ambitious], whether at home or absent, to be wellpleasing unto Him. For we must all be made manifest before the judgment seat of Christ; that each one may receive the things done in the body, according to what he hath done, whether it be good or bad." And here the Revisers scarcely do justice to their own text, in which *kakon* gives place to *phaulon*, whose primary meaning, according to Grimm, is "mean, worthless, of no account." As Archbishop Trench tells us in his *Synonyms of the New Testament*, "the notion of worthlessness is the central notion of *phaulos*."

When thus read aright, the passage refutes two rival errors which are sadly prevalent. The one, a legacy from certain of the Latin Fathers, challenges the truth of the Lord's words that the believer "cometh not into judgment," for the *bema* of Christ is not "the great white throne" of the Apocalyptic vision. And in the judgment of the redeemed the issue is not life or death, pardon or doom, but it relates to conduct and testimony while here below. And the rival error is that, in passing to heaven His people will receive a *lethé* draught which will destroy all memories of earth. This deplorable delusion robs the Christian life, not only of its solemnity, but of its significance, and it degrades heaven to the level of a fool's paradise. Moreover, as Bengel so well says: "The eternal remembrance of a great debt forgiven, will . . . foster . . . strongest love."[7]

In these days of excessive nerve strain, people fall into the hands of the police at times, not because of any wrong committed, but because they have been "found wandering." Who they are, they cannot tell, or where they come from. Their very name they have forgotten, and all their past is an utter blank. In a condition of this kind it is that Christians, not a few, expect to enter heaven!

Personality depends on memory; and if this whimsy of religious thought were a divine truth, death would mean annihilation for the Christian. My name may be in the book of life; but if death destroys all memories of earth, my identity with the *ego* who will bear that name in heaven is a mere theory, or, as the lawyers would say, "a legal fiction." And it has, for me, no interest, save as a subtle problem in metaphysics. It is not merely that my earthly friends will fail to recognize me; I shall not recognize myself! I shall be like one of the "found wandering" cases above referred to.

It may be said, perhaps, that it is only the evil of our present life that will be forgotten; the good will be remembered and rewarded. Is it possible that any Christian could cherish a thought so unworthy and so mean? It will be the remembrance of our *sins*—sins long forgotten, it may be—that will enable us to realize, as we never realized before, the wonders of divine love and grace, and the preciousness of the blood of our redemption. But further discussion is idle; for the teaching of our present verse is in the warp and woof of Bible doctrine on this subject.[8]

---

7. Bengel, *op. cit.*, p. 296.
8. 2 Cor. 5 is dealt with more fully in the author's book, *Forgotten Truths* (Grand Rapids: Kregel Publications, 1980).

*Now a Mediator is not of one but God is one* (Galatians 3:20).

In the *Speaker's Commentary*, Dean Howson remarks that "the interpretation of this verse is one of the curiosities of biblical criticism. The explanations of it are reckoned by hundreds" (Jowett mentions 430!). The following note, therefore, is offered merely by way of suggestions toward a correct interpretation of it.

The usual interpretation, adopted by eminent commentators, depends on construing the final word of the verse to mean "immutable." But though *eis* occurs nearly 250 times in the New Testament, it bears no such meaning anywhere else. And the suggestion that, in a brief and simple sentence like this, any writer would use one of the commonest of words in two wholly different senses, is so entirely without precedent or parallel that, if there be no other explanation open to us, we may well leave the passage unexplained. Moreover, this is not the only epistle in which the apostle emphasizes the truth that God is *one*. In 1 Corinthians 8:6, he writes, "To us there is but one God"; and in 1 Timothy 2:5, "For there is one God, and one mediator between God and men." Why then should we suppose that in Galatians the word is employed in a strange and mystical sense?

I venture to think the main difficulty in expounding the passage is due, not at all to the language of the twentieth verse, but to our putting on the words "covenant" and "mediator" a fixed meaning which they do not bear in the New Testament, or among Orientals generally. For it is assumed that a covenant is necessarily a compact between different parties, and that a mediator implies a covenant in that sense. But in his *Light from the Ancient East*, Professor Deissmann avers that *diathêkê* did not carry that meaning among Greek-speaking peoples in the first century.

And surely a study of this passage as a whole, and of verses 16 to 19 in particular, will make it clear that the apostle uses "covenant" and "promise" as convertible terms. It is noteworthy, moreover, that, in Grimm's *Lexicon*, the primary meaning of *diathêkê* is "a dispensation or arrangement of any sort, which one wishes to be valid." And it is as a secondary meaning that he gives "compact" and "covenant." Indeed, the question claims consideration whether, in the legal sense of the word, God ever made a covenant *with* men.

But, it will be asked, what of the Mosaic covenant? Here a suggestion of Bengel's is both interesting and important. It is that the Sinai covenant was not between *God* and the people; for "God delegated the law to angels as His representatives."[9] And in another passage he seems to say that the parties to that covenant were, on one side the law personified, and on the other the people, Moses being the mediator.

The word *mesitês* (mediator) occurs only once in the Septuagint (Job 31:31), and very seldom in pagan Greek writings. And in the New Testament, besides Galatians 3 and 1 Timothy 2:5, already noticed, it is used only in Hebrews 8:6, 9:15, and 12:24. Its use in Hebrews 8 in connection with covenant will throw light upon our present verse. What is the nature of the "better covenant" of which Christ is the mediator? The words are, "I will accomplish a new covenant upon the house of Israel" (v. 8).[10] And again, "This is the covenant that I will covenant to the house of Israel" (v. 10; repeated in 10:16). In these Hebrews passages, the apostle emphasizes the contrast between the Sinai compact and "the covenants of the promise"—to use his phrase in Ephesians 2:12 (R.V.). And is not this his purpose here also? The *law* covenant, as contrasted with the *promise* covenant, involved two parties, and the mediator of such a covenant represented both. But God is *one*, and there is no room in His promise covenant for a Mediator *in that sense*. For, as the *Lexicon* will tell us, the word has another meaning, namely, "a medium of communication." We all understand this in human affairs. The King's private Secretary, or his Secretary of State, is the *mesitês* through whom he deals with his subjects.

This leads me to suggest that the old-fashioned doctrine of "a redemption covenant between the persons of the Trinity" tended only to obscure and limit the great truth that, at no time, and in no circumstances, does God ever deal with men save in and through Christ. This truth led the old divines to

---

9. Bengel, *op. cit.*, p. 358.
10. See Revised Version margin. How can "*epi* with an accusative" be properly rendered "with"?

make Christ a party to the Sinai covenant —a view which, as above indicated, Scripture does not warrant. But whether it be a question of Israel's national blessings, or of the election and glory of the church the Body of Christ—whether it be a question of pardon and life for a repentant sinner, or of grace and guidance for a believer in his daily walk—all is in and through Christ. The ordinary meaning of *mesitês* is "a go-between"; and though we may not apply such a colloquial term to the Lord of Glory, the thought which it expresses is a right one. In His name it is that we pray for mercy and grace to help in time of need; and in and through Him it is that the mercy and the grace are given.

If then my view of the passage be right, the clue to a correct interpretation of it depends upon studying it in relation to the purpose with which it was written, namely, to refute the teaching of the Judaizers. They regarded the Abrahamic covenant as a covenant *with* "Abraham and his seed according to the flesh," and the Mosaic covenant as confirming and enlarging the peculiar privileges of Israel. And the reason why the ministry of Paul was specially obnoxious to them was because he was the apostle to and through whom was revealed the distinctive truth of grace, which ignored and swept away all special privileges of the kind. That truth he called "my gospel," for he regarded it as a special trust committed to him.

So his answer here was that the Abrahamic covenant was *to* the Patriarch and his "seed," and that it was not a compact or bargain, but a promise in grace, absolutely without condition; and that "the seed" of that covenant was not Israel, but Christ; and that the law, so far from confirming or extending this, "was added because of transgressions until the seed should come." It was on an altogether lower level—a compact arranged (*diatassô*) through angels by the hand of a mediator. "But a mediator [in that sense] is not of one," i.e., does not represent only one party; and therefore he could have no place in the *promise* covenant, in which God stood alone, for God is *one*.

*By grace are ye saved through faith; and that not of yourselves: it is the gift of God* (Ephesians 2:8).

"The gift of God" here intended is salvation by grace through faith. It is not the faith itself. "This is precluded," as Alford remarks, "by the manifestly parallel clauses 'not of yourselves' and 'not of works,' the latter of which would be irrelevant as asserted of faith."

It is still more definitely precluded by the character of the passage. It is *given* to us to believe on Christ, just in the same sense in which it is given to some "also to suffer for His sake" (Phil. 1:29). But the statement of our present verse is doctrinal; and in that sense the assertion that faith is a gift, or indeed that it is a distinct entity at all, is a sheer error. This matter is sometimes represented as though God first gives faith to the sinner, and then, on the sinner's bringing Him the faith, goes on to give him salvation! Just as though a baker, refusing to supply empty-handed applicants, should first dispense to each the price of a loaf, and then in return for the money out of his own pocket, serve out the bread! To answer fully such an oddity as that would need a treatise. Suffice it, therefore, to point out that to read the text as though faith were the gift, is to destroy not only the meaning of verse 9, but the force of the whole passage.[11]

*As truth is in Jesus* (Ephesians 4:21).

The popularity of the cant phrase, "the truth as it is in Jesus"— a perversion of this text—to express "Evangelical truth," or "the truth of Christ," is a signal proof that with Christians in general the Lord is named just as caprice or ignorance may suggest. In the narrative of the Gospels, those divine records of His earthly sojourn, the Lord is habitually called "Jesus." But the name of His humiliation is never used in this way in the Epistles. As Bishop Barry notices in commenting upon this very verse, "wherever it occurs in the epistles it will be found to be distinctive and emphatic."

This is strikingly exemplified in the two passages—and there are only two—in which He is thus named in the six later epistles of the apostle Paul.

---

11. This subject is fully dealt with in the author's book, *The Gospel and Its Ministry* (Grand Rapids: Kregel Publications, 1978).

In Philippians 2:9, 10, we read that "God hath given Him the name that is above every name, that at the name of Jesus every knee should bow." This can only mean that in the full realization that He is *Jesus*—the despised and rejected Galilean, He is to be acclaimed as Jehovah—"the name that is above every name that is named, not only in this world, but also in that which is to come" (Eph. 1:21). And in our present text (as appears so plainly from the verses which precede and follow it), it is not *doctrine* the apostle has in view, but practical Christian living. Referring to the base immoralities of the Gentiles, he writes, "But not so did ye learn Christ; if indeed it was He that ye heard, and in Him that ye were taught, according as is truth in Jesus" (Alford)—in other words, the truth as exemplified in His life on earth in the time of His humiliation.

> *Wives, submit yourselves unto your own husbands, as unto the Lord* (Ephesians 5:22 ff.).

In this section of Ephesians the marriage relationship is read-justed by a heavenly standard, the ordinance of Genesis 2:24 being reenacted on a spiritual basis and with a new sanction. The church is the body of Christ, and "because we are members of His Body" (v. 80, R.V.) the Christian is "to love his wife *even as himself.*" For while the bridal relationship which pertains to the heavenly election out of Israel implies the closest unity, the *body* relationship between Christ and the church connotes absolute oneness. And this is the "great mystery" of verse 32; not the marriage bond—for such a use of the word "mystery" is foreign to Scripture—but the truth of the one body, which is especially revealed in this epistle. And so the apostle adds, "I am speaking concerning Christ and the Church. Nevertheless (*plēn, i.e.* though it is not true in fact of man and wife, yet because it is true of Christ and the church) let every one of you so love his wife even as himself."

How is it conceivable that, if the church-bride doctrine were a divine truth, the apostle would not have made it the basis of this exhortation? But that doctrine is discredited by the absence of all mention of it in this the very Scripture which is supposed to teach it. It may be said, perhaps, that verse 27 implies it. But the body figure expresses a corporate unity, and until it is complete it cannot be presented. It is now only in building (4:12, 13). In Revelation 19:7 we have a kindred thought in the bride becoming ready. The church-bride doctrine is really a by-product of that deplorable error of Patristic theology, that God *has* "cast away His people whom He foreknew"; and therefore their promised blessings are now appropriated by the church! The question whether A. B. is C. D.'s wife may receive a negative answer, either by pointing to another woman as his wife, or by indicating a relationship between them which is incompatible with marriage. And in both ways Scripture vetoes the church-bride theory. For Abraham's city, the heavenly Jerusalem, is the bride, and that city is "our mother"! (Gal. 4:26, R.V.). It may be added that the typology of Scripture refutes it. For Isaac was admittedly a type of Christ, and it was the divine purpose that his bride should be of his own kindred.[12]

But it may be asked, As these body and bride phrases are figurative, may they not be interchangeable? We must here distinguish between a figure which expresses a truth, as when the Lord called Himself "the Shepherd of the sheep," and a figure which is merely illustrative, as when He said He was the Door of the sheep. And the figures of the body and the bride are in the former category, and express real relationships.

We may learn much by marking the order in which these truths appear in the New Testament. The bride is prominently mentioned in the kingdom ministry (John 3:29); but during all the interval between the close of that ministry and the Patmos visions, Israel is set aside and the bride disappears from Scripture. Is it conceivable that if the church were really the Bride we should seek in vain for a single mention of it, or even of the word *numphê* throughout that entire section of Scripture in which the truth of the church is specially revealed?

The use made of 2 Corinthians 9:2 in this connection is a strange oddity of exegesis. In his *Sketches of Jewish Social Life in the Days of Christ*,[13] Dr. Alfred Edersheim cites the passage to illustrate the functions of "the friend of the bridegroom." But to

---

12. To interpret verse 31 in a carnal sense is an outrage upon Scripture.
13. Alfred Edersheim, *Sketches of Jewish Social Life in the Days of Christ* (Grand Rapids: Wm. B. Eerdmans Publishing Co.).

construe such an illustrative reference as being a divine revelation of a truth of such vital importance betrays want of respect both for Holy Scripture and for the intelligence of men.[14] Moreover, if the Christians of Corinth were the Bride of Christ, the same must have been true of every other local church; and if thus construed, the verse would suggest a *harem* rather than a wife! And by a single step further in error the Church of Rome applies it to the individual, and thus claims a scriptural sanction for the evil system of convents and nuns.

And this should bar our dismissing this subject with a *cui bono*? All Scripture is profitable *if read aright*. But perverted Scripture has been the bane of Christianity. For by a misuse of Scripture the historic church has found a warrant for every atrocity and crime that has befouled its history. And if every true Christian ought to stand clear of its guilt, this responsibility rests especially upon any one who brings the gospel to Jews; and if he ignores or shirks it he is false to his message and his Lord. It behooves him to declare, in the spirit of Dean Alford's words quoted on page 36, that "the Christian Church . . . the outward frame of Christendom" is an apostasy, and to remind his hearers that the Christian victims of its fiendish persecutions have outnumbered the Jewish a hundredfold.

More than that, it behooves him to repudiate that "orthodox" system of exegesis which, by spiritualizing the prophetic Scriptures, robs the covenant people of their heritage—an evil system which, as Adolf Saphir wrote, "has paved the way for Rationalism and Neology." And he might begin with the twenty-first chapter of Revelation. Can we not realize the wondering delight of a company of Jews on hearing for the first time the glowing words of the Patmos vision of the heavenly Jerusalem, and being told by a Christian preacher that it is all for Israel, and will be realized for Israel in the coming age, when at last they accept their long-rejected Messiah!

*Work out your own salvation* (Philippians 2:12).

This phrase has passed into common use. And, strange to

---

14. There is no mention of "bride" in the passage. The apostle uses the ordinary word for an unmarried girl.

say, on the secular page it seems always to represent a true thought, whereas in "Christian" use it often implies a denial of "salvation by grace"—that great fundamental truth of Christianity.

Many an error is due to the habit of putting a theological label upon New Testament words, and then reading that meaning into every passage where they occur. The word *sôtêria* means "safety" or "deliverance," and the context must always guide us as to the nature of the peril referred to. In Acts 7:25, for example, the word has reference to Israel's bondage in Egypt; in Hebrews 11:7 to the judgment of the Flood; and in Acts 27:34 to the foundering of the ship in which Paul was being conveyed to Rome. To the ordinary reader of our Authorized Version the apostle's words, "This is for your health," must appear grotesquely incongruous; for when men are face to face with death it is *not* their health they think about, but their safety; and *sôtêria* is the word here used.

It is noteworthy, moreover, that although the apostle had an explicit divine promise that there would be no loss of life (v. 24), he impressed on the men the need of taking food to fit them for the struggle for life which awaited them. This is of great practical importance in these days when, in sickness, for instance, "the use of means" is condemned by some as though it implied want of faith in God. Isaiah was divinely commissioned to bring King Hezekiah the definite promise that he would recover from his malignant disease; and yet he ordered the use of the best remedy known in those days (2 Kings 20:1-7).[15]

It is in its ordinary sense that the apostle uses the word *sôtêria* in Philippians 1:19. This does not mean that his hope of eternal salvation was enhanced by the fact that evil men were preaching Christ, "supposing to add affliction to his hands"; but he hailed it as likely to increase his prospect of an acquittal at his impending trial. In our ignorance of all the circumstances we are unable to appreciate this, but the issue proved that he was right.

Thus in 2:12 he was thinking of the spiritual perils by which

---

15. See note on James 4:14, *post.*

his beloved Philippians were beset; and he appealed to them
by their loyalty to himself, and by the fact of his enforced absence, to work out their own deliverance. The explanation which
refers this to their salvation in the theological sense rings the
changes upon "working out" and "working in." But this is a
play upon the wording of our English translation. The contrast
implied in the phrase "work out *your own* deliverance" is an
absolute bar to any such exegesis. For, if thus read, the apostle's
words must mean, either that they were to work out their own,
instead of other people's, salvation; or else to secure their own
salvation, instead of trusting him to do it for them. And as
regards *eternal* salvation, both these alternatives are obviously
false. His words to the Ephesians were no less true to the Philippians: "By grace are ye saved through faith; and that [salva-
tion] not of yourselves: it is the gift of God" (Eph. 2:8; see pp.
92-93, *ante*). And the struggle to which he called them was akin
to that in view of which he enjoined upon the Ephesians to put
on the whole armor of God—a struggle to be maintained "in
fear and trembling" to the end.

*If by any means I might attain unto the resurrection of the
dead* (Philippians 3:11).

If the commonly received exegesis of this passage be correct,
we are faced by the astounding fact that the author of the
Epistle to the Romans and of the fifteenth chapter of 1 Corinthians—the apostle who was in a peculiar sense entrusted with
the supreme revelation of grace—announced when nearing the
close of his ministry that the resurrection was not, as he had
been used to teach, a blessing which divine grace assured to all
believers in Christ, but a prize to be won by the sustained
efforts of a life of wholly exceptional saintship.

Nor is this all. In the same epistle he has already said, "To
me to live is Christ, and to have died is gain," whereas, *ex hypothesi*, it now appears that his chief aim was to earn a right to the
resurrection, and that death, instead of bringing gain, would
have cut him off before he had reached the standard of saintship
needed to secure that prize! For his words are explicit, "Not as
though I had already attained."

Here was one who was not a least bit behind the chiefest apostles; who excelled them all in labors and sufferings for his Lord, and in the visions and revelations accorded to him; whose prolonged ministry, moreover, was accredited by mighty signs and wonders, by the power of the Spirit of God. And yet, being now "such an one as Paul the aged," he was in doubt whether he should have part in that resurrection which he had taught all his Corinthian converts to hope for and expect.

Such is the exposition of the apostle's teaching in many a standard commentary. And yet the passage which is thus perverted reaches its climax in the words, "Our citizenship is in heaven, from whence we are looking for the Savior, the Lord Jesus Christ, who shall fashion anew the body of our humiliation that it may be conformed to the body of His glory" (Phil. 3:20, 21).

"Our citizenship is in heaven." Here is the clue to the teaching of the whole passage. The truth to which his words refer is more clearly stated in Ephesians 2:6, "God has quickened us together with Christ, and raised us up with Him, and made us sit with Him in the heavenly places in Christ." More clearly still is it given in Colossians 3:1-3, "If then ye were raised together with Christ, seek the things that are above, where Christ is, seated on the right hand of God. Set your mind on the things that are above, not on the things on the earth. For ye died, and your life is hid with Christ in God."

Ephesians and Colossians, be it remembered, were written at the same period of his ministry as Philippians; and in the light of these Scriptures we can read this chapter aright. To win Christ (v. 8), or to apprehend, or lay hold of, that for which he had been laid hold of, or apprehended (v. 12)—or in other words, to realize practically in his life on earth what was true of him doctrinally as to his standing before God in heaven—this is what he was reaching toward, and what he says he had not already attained.

The high calling of verse 14 is interpreted by some to mean Christ's calling up His own to meet Him in the air (a blessing assured to all "who are alive and remain unto the coming of the Lord"), but this is not in keeping with the plain words: God's high calling in Christ Jesus, i.e. what God has called us (made us) to be in Christ.

If the passage refers to the literal resurrection, then the words, "not as though I had already attained," must mean that, while here on earth and before the Lord's coming, the apostle hoped either to undergo the change of verse 21, or else to win some sort of saintship diploma, or certificate, to ensure his being raised at the second coming of Christ. These alternatives are inexorable; and they only need to be stated to ensure their rejection.

One word more. If the apostle Paul, after such a life of saintship and service, was in doubt as to his part in the resurrection, no one of us, unless indeed he be the proudest of Pharisees or the blindest of fools, will dream of attaining it.[16]

> *Them which sleep in Jesus will God bring with Him*
> (1 Thessalonians 4:14).

The passage from which these words are quoted is a "misunderstood text," partly on account of inaccurate translation, and partly because it is read on the text-card system. "Sleeping in Jesus" is a phrase which, though enshrined in religious thought, is not warranted by Scripture. The primary meaning of the verb *koimaô* is not "to sleep," but "to cause to sleep" or "to put to sleep" (Grimm's *Lexicon*). And that this is its meaning here is indicated by the fact that it is followed by *dia*. For no one with an elementary knowledge of Greek will need the R.V. marginal note to tell him that *dia* means "through" or "by." There is no ambiguity in the apostle's words. And when read in the light of the epistle as a whole, and of the narrative of the Book of Acts, their significance is clear. The "dead in Christ" of verse 16 is a general term which includes all departed saints. But verse 14 refers to "the sleeping ones" of verse 13—for such is the literal rendering of *koimômentôn* —certain definitely known individuals whose death the Thessalonian saints were mourning.

The duration of the apostle's visit to Thessalonica is not recorded. His synagogue ministry lasted only three weeks (Acts

---

16. *Exanastasis*, which is the word here used, occurs nowhere else in the New Testament. And this fact surely strengthens the presumption that the apostle is here treating of the resurrection in a peculiar sense.

17:2); but his stay must have been much more prolonged. For such "a great multitude" of Greeks believed (v. 4) that the church was essentially Gentile (1 Thess. 1:9). Moreover, their faith and their testimony were already spoken of far and wide (v. 8). It was evidently the success of the apostle's mission, after he had turned his back upon the Synagogue, which excited the jealousy of the Jews, and led to the riot which compelled him to find safety in flight. After a very brief ministry in Berea, he passed on to Athens. While there, such grave tidings reached him from Thessalonica that he sent Timothy back, and it was the report which Timothy brought, when he rejoined the apostle at Corinth, that supplied the groundwork of 1 Thessalonians.

The Epistle discloses the cause of the trouble. Certain of their leaders had been martyred (2:14-16). "Leaders," I say, because in every persecution the leaders are the first to fall. But had they not been taught that He under whose banner they enlisted was the Lord of Glory, who had all power in heaven and on earth? Were they to conclude then that this teaching was untrue? Or was it that their martyrs had been cut off because of divine displeasure, thus causing them to mourn their death "even as others who have no hope"?

We fail to appreciate the fears and difficulties of the Gentile converts of early days. The faith of the spiritual Christian who has the Bible in his hands, and to whom the story of the church's sufferings is an open page, may pierce the darkest clouds; but these Thessalonians had no such glorious records of a faith-tried past; and it is doubtful to what extent they had access even to the Hebrew Scriptures. And in this connection the fact is noteworthy that it is not to the Scriptures the apostle appears, but to public facts respecting Jewish hate and resulting martyrdoms (ch. 2:14-16).

But the epistle was more than a word of exhortation and comfort from their spiritual father; it conveyed a special message from the Lord Himself. For such is the force of the words, "This we are saying unto you in the word of the Lord" (4:15). "I tell you this as a message straight from the Lord" is the interpretation given in Bishop Ellicott's *New Testament Commentary*.

This explains the mode in which Christ is named in the fourteenth verse. For had the apostle been speaking as from himself he would, according to his invariable practice, have called Him the Lord, as he does five times in this very passage. The trouble in the Thessalonian church was that their loved ones had been put to death on account of their testimony for Christ. Was He not then responsible for their death? The Lord, as it were, accepts the charge. He it was who had put them to sleep; and in exquisite grace He tells them so in the name of His humiliation—the name in which He Himself had been put to death. As surely as He died and rose again, so surely would they whom they were mourning rise again. And they would be at no disadvantage. The living would have no precedence; for the mourners and the mourned would be caught up together in the clouds to meet the Lord. This was the first message the Lord gave to saints on earth after His ascension. Revelation 22:16 records the latest. And in both He speaks in the name of His humiliation.

These notes are exegetical; but on this subject there are certain considerations that cannot be denied expression. First, the correctness and simplicity of the language of Holy Scripture about death. The Christian dies in the Lord (Rev. 14:13); or, by an exquisite euphemism, he falls asleep in Christ (1 Cor. 15:18). Why then should we resort to the non-Scriptural phrases now so popular with Christians? Secondly, the misreading of the Lord's words in our present verse has robbed us of the truth that if Christians lose their lives for His sake, He claims that it is He Himself who "puts them to sleep." And thirdly, the definiteness with which the early saints were taught to regard His Coming as a present hope. Surely, therefore, the question whether His Coming is to be "premillennial" should be placed in the same category as whether He was born of a virgin, and whether His death was "for our sins, according to the Scriptures."[17]

---

17. The foregoing note is based upon the author's book, *Forgotten Truths* (Grand Rapids: Kregel Publications, 1980).

*We beseech you, brethren, by the coming of our Lord Jesus
Christ, and our gathering together unto Him, that ye be not
soon shaken in mind, . . . as that the day of Christ is at hand*
(2 Thessalonians 2:1, 2).

The error which this epistle was written to refute is embod-
ied in the beliefs of Christendom. It is the error of supposing
that the Lord Jesus will never again come from heaven until
after "the great tribulation" of Messianic prophecy. It is a view
held very firmly even by many spiritual Christians, and held
with all the bitterness of controversy by not a few.

The question arises, how such an error could have taken
hold of the Thessalonians, seeing that they had the apostle's
first epistle in their hands. The answer is that it was not in their
hands. Some trusted individuals doubtless had it in safe keeping. But their prominent leaders had been martyred in the persecution then raging, and the mass of the converts must have
been dependent on what they remembered of it from hearing it
read "in church." It is highly doubtful, moreover, whether in a
time of such fierce persecution they could assemble on the
Lord's day. The probability is that at such a time they could
only meet furtively, and in small and scattered groups (see
note on 1 Thess. 4:14).

Moreover, if the generally accepted explanation of 2 Thessalonians 2:2 and 3:17 be correct, they had received a forged
letter, purporting to come from the apostle, which seemed to
modify or cancel his previous teaching. Nowadays the error is
defended by a misreading of Matthew 24; but it is improbable
that the Thessalonians had any written records of the Lord's
personal teaching. That teaching, however, referred definitely
to Hebrew prophecy about "the great tribulation"; and the Hebrew converts among them would have had knowledge of
such Scriptures as Malachi 4:5, Isaiah 13, and Joel 2; for the
reading of a lesson from the prophets was a part of the sabbath
service of the synagogue. We can understand then how easily
they could have glided into the error of supposing that the
persecution then raging was the "tribulation" of prophecy. And
this would lead to the further error about "the day of the
Lord"—for this, and not "the day of Christ," is the approved
reading of the text.

This second epistle then was written to correct these errors, and to calm the fears to which they gave rise. And the apostle's appeal is based on the great truth which his first epistle had impressed upon them, namely, "the coming of our Lord Jesus Christ, and our gathering together unto Him." The day of the Lord was neither present (R.V.) nor at hand (A.V.). For, as He had told them while yet with them, that day would not come till after the apostasy, and the revelation of the Man of Sin.

The apostle's words, "I beseech you *on behalf of* the coming of our Lord Jesus Christ" (R.V. margin), show clearly that the error against which he was warning them was destructive of the truth he had taught them. They could not live looking for that blessed hope (Titus 2:13) if they were living in expectation of the awful terrors of "the tribulation" and "the day of the Lord." For these lines of truth are wholly separate. The one is the line of Messianic prophecy, leading up to the coming of Christ as Son of Man in a future age, for the deliverance of His earthly people, and the establishment of His earthly kingdom. The other is not within the range of Messianic prophecy at all, but points to the fulfilment of the heavenly hope of His heavenly people of this Christian dispensation.[18] It is not strange, moreover, that in those early days when the Christians had no Testaments or Bibles in their homes to refer to, the very peculiar circumstances of the Thessalonian converts should have led them to fall into error on the subject. But strange it is, surely, and as sad as it is strange, that, in the full light of the Christian revelation, an error should prevail, which ignores or denies such all-important and distinctive truth of that revelation. But, alas! "the churches have forgotten the hope of the church."

*Let these also first be proved; then let them serve as deacons, if they be blameless* (1 Timothy 3:10, R.V.).

In his commentary on 1 Timothy 3, Dean Alford says tersely that "the *episkopoi* of the New Testament have officially nothing in common with our bishops." And he might have said also that, when the New Testament was written, the Greek lan-

---

18. See p. 15, *ante,* and also the notes on 1 Corinthians 15 and 1 Thessalonians 4.

guage had no special word to correspond with our "deacon." For *diakonos* is a generic word for servant. It was used both of household servants and of ministers of the gospel; and the apostle Paul applied it to himself, and even to Christ. Our text, therefore, is misunderstood only because it is mistranslated. The noun is *diakonos* and the verb is *diakoneô*. In another connection, therefore, it would be rendered, "Let the servants be proved, and if found blameless let them serve"; here, of course, it should read, "Let the ministers be proved, and if found blameless let them minister." Some men were apostolically appointed to "the office of a bishop"; but ministers were, like the apostles themselves, the gift of Christ,[19] and they are included in that category in Ephesians 4:7-11. It is noteworthy that in that passage, seeing that it deals with the vital unity of the Body of Christ, no mention is made of "governments"; for rule has to do with the visible church on earth, to which 1 Corinthians 12:28 refers. No less noteworthy is it that, though teachers are specified in both, for their ministry obviously has reference to both, evangelists have no place in 1 Corinthians 12, for the sphere of their ministry is not the church, but the world.

Philippians 1:1, which is the only other passage where the word "deacon" occurs in our English versions, ought of course to read "bishops and ministers." Although etymologically and in their origin "minister" and "deacon" are synonymous, the word "deacon" has acquired such a definitely distinctive meaning that its retention by the revisers is a flagrant violation of their avowed principles, due, no doubt, to their reluctance to discredit the figment that the *diakonos* was a subordinate office-bearer in the church. Such an error is sufficiently refuted by the fact, already noticed, that the apostle Paul uses the word of himself seven times; and in Romans 15:8 he applies it to the Lord Jesus Christ.

It is noteworthy that in Scripture the word is not used of Stephen and his fellows, whose appointment "to serve tables"

---

19. This truth survives in the service for "making of deacons" (*i.e.* ministers). For, before ordaining a candidate, the Bishop demands whether he thinks he is called to the ministry "according to the will of our Lord Jesus Christ." The church on earth may appoint to *office*, but in the case of the *gift*, its function is merely to recognize it.

is recorded in Acts 6. It is also noteworthy that, as Dr. Hatch has indicated in his great work, *The Organization of the Early Christian Churches*, the duties thus assigned to them devolved upon the bishops when the church was fully organized.

> *Who gave Himself for us, that He might . . . purify unto Himself a peculiar people, zealous of good work* (Titus 2:14).

"A peculiar people." The popular reading of this phrase not only misses important truth, but it has a sinister influence upon many a Christian life. The word *periousios* occurs nowhere else in the New Testament; but it is taken from the Greek version of Exodus 9:5: "All the earth is Mine, but ye shall be to Me a peculiar people above all nations." And our English word admirably expresses the sense of the original. For, as the dictionary tells us, "*peculiar* is from the Roman *peculium*, which was a thing emphatically and distinctively one's own, and hence was dear."

To be "a peculiar people," then, is not to be a people with uncouth or eccentric manners and ways. It is to be emphatically and distinctively God's own people in a wholly special sense, and therefore to be very specially dear to Him.

> *According to His mercy He saved us, by the washing of regeneration and renewing of the Holy Ghost* (Titus 3:5).

The usual exposition of this verse exemplifies the practice of putting theological labels upon New Testament words, and then reading the passage as thus perverted. Each of the prominent words here used occurs but once again in the New Testament: "renewing," in Romans 12:2; "regeneration," in Matthew 19:28; and "washing," in Ephesians 5:26.

The word rendered "washing" is *loutron*, not a verb, but a noun. It is, strictly speaking, not the washing, but the vessel which contains the water. Certain expositors, of course, wish to read it "font" or "laver"; but this is a false exegesis. The New Testament is written in the language of the Greek version of the Old, and we turn to that authority to settle for us the meaning of any doubtful term. And for this purpose the Apocryphal books are sometimes as useful as the sacred Scriptures. Now, *loutron* is not the rendering for "laver" in the Greek version. The LXX uses it twice; namely, in Canticles 4:2 (where it is the washing-place for sheep); and in Ecclesiasticus 34:25, where the Son of Sirach writes, "He that washes himself after the touching of a dead body, if he touch it again, what avails his *loutron*?"

This last passage is of the very highest importance here, for it gives us the clue for which we search. The reference is to one of the principal ordinances of the Mosaic ritual—a type, moreover, which fills a large place in New Testament doctrine, and very specially in Hebrews; namely, the great sin-offering as connected with the water of purification (Num. 19).

The absence of both preposition and article before "renewing" requires that the words should be construed together— "the *loutron* of regeneration and renewing of the Holy Spirit." The reference here is not to a mystical doctrine adopted in aftertimes by the church in its decadence, but to one of the greatest of the types of the divinely ordered Hebrew religion. The great sin offering of Numbers 19 was burned outside the camp, and water which had flowed over the ashes had cleansing efficacy.

But does Scripture connect that type with the Spirit's work? First, let us note that in Matthew 19:28—the only other passage where the word "regeneration" is used—it refers to the fulfillment of the kingdom blessings to Israel, the epoch described in Acts 3:21 as "the times of the restoration of all things, which God hath spoken by the mouth of all His holy prophets." With this clue to guide us, we turn to one of the most definite of these prophecies, Ezekiel 36 and 37. We read, "I will take you from among the heathen, and gather you out of all countries, and will bring you into your own land. *Then will I sprinkle clean water upon you . . . A new heart also will I give you . . . And I will put My Spirit within you.*" Then follows the vision of the valley full of dry bones. The prophet is commanded to say, "Thus saith the Lord God, come from the four winds, O Breath, and breathe upon these slain, that they may live." And once again the words are repeated, "I will put My Spirit in you, and ye shall live."

Here, then, is the most characteristic of all the prophecies of that great revival which the Lord described as "the regenera-tion"—a prophecy to which the Jew clung with special earnest-ness. And it was the great truth of this prophecy—salvation through the sin-offering in the power of the divine Spirit—that the Lord enforced in His words to Nicodemus.[20]

Now, let us turn to the General Epistles to discover what awaits us there. . . .

---

20. See note on John 3:5, *ante.*

# 5

## *Misunderstood Texts in the General Epistles*

*For every high priest taken from among men is ordained for men in things pertaining to God, that he may offer both gifts and sacrifices for sins* (Hebrews 5:1).

A sufficient reason for including this verse in a list of "misunderstood texts" is supplied by the fact that the revisers' "correction" of our Authorized Version attributes to the apostle two statements which are directly opposed to the teaching of the epistle. Here is their reading of it: "For every high priest, being taken from among men, is appointed for men in things pertaining to God, that he may offer both gifts and sacrifices for sins."[1] But 4:1 states emphaticaly that our "great High Priest" is not "taken from among men," but that He is the Son of God. And in the sequel we are told no less emphaticallly that it was not until after His ascension that He was "called of God a High Priest." The word here rendered "called" occurs nowhere else in Scripture. It signifies that God then "proclaimed and constituted" Him High Priest (Bloomfield).

---

1. A parable may illustrate their blunder. An army manual reads, "Every commissioned officer raised from the ranks is promoted for valor or special merit." But an ignorant editor "corrects" it to say, "Every commissioned officer, being raised from the ranks, is promoted for . . ."

But our present verse declares that, in contrast with the priesthood of Christ, "every high priest *taken from among men* is appointed to offer gifts and sacrifices for sins." "An antithesis to Christ, for the apostle is here speaking of the Levitical priesthood."[2] "The high priest is here described as selected from among men. involving a tacit comparison with the divine High Priest" (Bloomfield). And the Lord is a priest after the order of Melchisedec, a priesthood that has nothing to do with offering gifts and sacrifices for sins. The English phrase, indeed, would seem to permit of a distinction between His offering gifts and His offering sacrifices for sins. But the Greek will not permit of this (Alford).

The fact that our High Priest is the Son of God might seem to separate Him from frail and erring mortals such as we are. But mark the words of the passage. In the epistles of the New Testament the Holy Spirit never speaks of the Lord Jesus Christ by His human name—the name of His humiliation—save with some special significance. And so here it is "Jesus, the Son of God." It is because He is the Son of God that His priesthood avails us, but it is our joy to remember that He is the "Jesus" of the humiliation, who can be "touched with the feeling of our infirmities, for He was in all points tried as we are."

*It is impossible . . . to renew them again unto repentance*
(Hebrews 6:4-6).

Although we can all distinguish between Christianity and the religion of Christendom, we are apt to miss the still clearer distinction between Judaism regarded as the divine religion and as "the Jews' religion." The divine religion pointed to Christ, and was fulfilled in Him, but the Jews' religion crucified Christ. That in our day evangelical Christians should turn to altars and priests, is not only anti-Christian, but in every respect contemptible. But we fail to realize what a hold the outward symbols and ceremonies of their historic cult must have had upon the Hebrew Christians, and how natural it was that they should

---

2. John Bengel, *Bengel's New Testament Commentary*, vol. 2, p. 610.

cling to them. What need there must have been for warnings and appeals such as those of Hebrews 6!

A chief function of the groomsman, or (to use the Oriental phrase) "the friend of the bridegroom," was to present the bride to him. But if the bride turned to follow the groomsman when, after fulfilling his duty, he withdrew, she would be regarded as a wanton, and treated as an outcast. And this may illustrate the apostasy of those who turn back to "religion" after coming to Christ. "They crucify to themselves the Son of God afresh" (v. 6). It is not that in fact they do this, any more than a man would really murder his brother because of hating him. And the apostle very definitely acknowledges this in verse 9. But God judges a path by the goal to which it leads; and it behooves His people to accept, and be guided by, the divine estimate of their thoughts and deeds. And this is the purpose of the sixth chapter of Hebrews. It is a perversion of it to treat it as intended to limit or undermine the believer's confidence, or his sense of security in Christ. Indeed, no passage in the epistle is better fitted to confirm and establish faith than that which immediately follows the warning words of these earlier verses of chapter 6.

*For this He did once, when He offered up Himself* (Hebrews 7:27).

It is not "the poor of the flock" only who need to be told that the word "once" here means "once for all," and not "once upon a time." For if this had not been ignored by the wise and prudent, the Christendom ordinance of the Mass would never have been instituted.

The word *ephapax* is used but five times in the New Testament, and only by the apostle Paul. In Hebrews 9:12 we read that Christ "entered into the holy place once for all, having obtained eternal redemption"; and in 10:10, "we have been sanctified through the offering of the body of Jesus Christ once for all." And Romans 6:10 tells us that "He died unto sin once for all." Though not a few Roman Catholics have a saving knowledge of Christ, they never enjoy settled peace, because they know nothing of a "once-for-all" sacrifice, and an eternal redemption. And the same is true of many a Protestant.

First Corinthians 15: 6 is the only other passage where *ephapax* occurs. And the apostle's use of the word generally may well support a doubt as to whether we read it aright in taking it to mean merely that the "more than five hundred brethren" who saw the Lord on the mountain in Galilee were all present at the same time. For the apostle's purpose is to put on record the human evidence for the Resurrection. And as a matter of *evidence* the proof would have been immeasurably stronger if every one of the five hundred had received a separate and independent vision of the Lord. May not the passage mean that this was a "once-for-all" manifestation of Himself to His assembled disciples as representatives of all who should afterwards believe in Him.

> *Unto them that look for Him shall He appear the second time, without sin, unto salvation* (Hebrews 9:28).

As these words are usually read on "the text-card system," and without reference to the context, they are supposed to refer to the so-called "Second Advent"—a phrase which, both in theological literature and in popular use, points to the dread *dies irae* of a remote future. When a phrase has thus acquired a definitely distinctive meaning, it savors of pedantry to use it in any other sense. And as this particular phrase embodies and perpetuates a gross error of patristic teaching, which would rob us of the Christian hope of the Lord's coming, we shall do well to discard it. For if Christ's "coming to judge the world" be His *second* coming, the sceptic has good ground for asserting that the coming revealed in the epistles—"that blessed hope"—is a superstitious belief based upon apostolic ignorance.

As noticed on a preceding page,[3] the Second Advent of theology will be the fourth or fifth coming of Christ. But what especially concerns us here is that there is no reference to it in Hebrews 9:28, which speaks of His appearing a second time for salvation. And it is noteworthy that this word "appear" is the ordinary word for "being seen," and is so translated in 1 Corinthians 15:5, 6, 7, and 8. It is wholly different from the word

---

3. See page 20, *ante.*

used respecting the Lord's coming in 1 Timothy 6:14; 2 Timothy 1:10 and 4:1, 8; and in Titus 2:13. Our verse therefore might be rendered, "By them who look for Him He will be seen a second time" ("*the* second time" is a mistranslation, due no doubt to the influence of the "Second Advent" doctrine).

But the burden of this section of Hebrews is the doctrine of the sin offering. And the closing words of chapter 9 would bring vividly to the mind of a Hebrew Christian the ritual of the Day of Atonement. Upon that red-letter day of Israel's sacred calendar, the High Priest offered the great yearly sin-offering, and when the prescribed ritual in all its parts was fulfilled, he passed within the veil; and the assembled Israelites watched and waited until he reappeared to bless them. For his thus reappearing was a pledge and proof that the sacrifice was accepted and expiation accomplished.

The accuracy of the type is absolute. Why was Aaron commanded to put off his high priestly garments before offering the sin offering, and not to wear them again until after he had entered the divine presence with the blood? Why, but because it was not until after the Ascension, when, having "put away sin by the sacrifice of Himself" (v. 26), and, having passed into the heavens "by His own blood," that Christ was "called of God a High Priest." And while Aaron's appearing again in his garments of glory and beauty to bless the people will have, in the antitype, a literal fulfilment for the earthly people of the covenant, the heavenly election of this dispensation have not to await that "second time" appearing. For to them it is given by faith to "enter into the holiest" by that same blood by which He entered there, and thus to behold Him apart from sin and sin offerings.[4]

Dispensationally, this part of the type will be fulfilled in a definite way to the elect remnant of Israel, who will be looking for their Messiah; but in its spiritual teaching it is a truth for every believer. For though the death of Christ, as the antitype of the sin offering, is in God's sight the ground of our peace, our own appreciation of His sacrifice, and our realization of the

---

4. *Chôris amartias.* It is not clear whether the word "sin" is not here used for sin offering, as in Hebrews 10:6, 8, and 18.

peace it gives, depends upon our seeing Him by faith apart
from sin. It is the Hebrews aspect of the truth which Romans
connects with the resurrection of Christ. And it is truth which
has no place in the cult of the crucifix. Therefore is it that,
although many Roman Catholics may have a spiritual knowledge of Christ, they never seem to enjoy settled peace.

A right understanding of this Hebrews passage will prevent
its being misused to support the figment that, at the coming of
the Lord, none will be "caught up" save those who will be
"looking for Him." If this were true, multitudes of spiritual
Christians would be left behind. For are they not earnestly
warned by their spiritual teachers that they ought to live looking, not for Christ, but for Antichrist and all the horrors and
terrors which, as the Lord declared in Matthew 24, must precede His coming as Son of Man, for the deliverance of His
earthly people in a future age?

*If we sin wilfully . . . there remaineth no more sacrifice for*
*sins* (Hebrews 10:26 ff.).

The preceding note on Hebrews 6:4-6 leaves but little to be
said upon this kindred passage. And that little cannot be better
expressed than in the words of Dean Alford's *Commentary*. The
sin here meant, he says, is "the sin of apostasy from Christ back
to the state which preceded the reception of Christ, namely,
Judaism. This is the ground-sin of all other sins. The verb is in
the present, not the past. 'If we be found wilfully sinning,' not
'if we have wilfully sinned,' at that day. It is not of an act, or of
any number of acts of sin, that the writer is speaking, which
might be repented of and blotted out; but of a state of sin in
which a man is found when that day shall come."

Here, moreover, as in chapter 6, the immediate sequel plainly indicates that nothing was further from the apostle's purpose
than to limit or weaken the faith of the Hebrew Christians. And
it further confirms the view that the warning had reference, not
to lapses in the sphere of morals, but to "drawing back" to the
religion that was fulfilled in Christ. And if such words were
needed in the case of those who were turning back to the divine religion of Judaism, what a voice they should have for
those who turn to the sham altars of Christianized paganism!

The prevalence of altars in our churches today is a sad and signal proof that there has been a grievous lapse from the faith of Christ during the last half century. And it is all the more strange, because "to recognize an altar in a Christian place of worship is to run counter to the doctrines of the Church of England . . . That the Reformers wished to discountenance the notion of altars appears from the fact that, at the Reformation, altars were ordered to be called tables; because, as Bishop Hooper said, 'as long as altars remain, both the ignorant people and the ignorant and evil-minded priest will always dream of sacrifice.'"[5]

What concerns us more closely here, however, is that *Christianity* knows nothing of altars. Moreover, "the only priests under the gospel, designated as such in the New Testament, are the saints, the members of the Christian brotherhood. As individuals, all Christians are priests alike."[6]

*We have an altar whereof they have no right to eat which serve the Tabernacle* (Hebrews 13:10).

The popular exposition of this verse depends on emphasizing the pronouns in order to make it indicate a contrast between Christianity and Judaism. But in the original Greek the pronouns are not expressed. If they were, we might convey their force in an English translation by printing them in italics. For example, a Roman Catholic might say, "*We* have an altar," thus implying a contrast with Protestants who have none. But without the emphasis, the phrase thus addressed to Hebrew Christians is equivalent to "There is an altar." And this is here the force of the apostle's words. For he is not propounding a new Christian doctrine, but illustrating and enforcing the practical truth which finds definite expression in the thirteenth verse. And with this end in view, he refers to ordinances of the divine religion of Judaism, with which every Hebrew Christian was familiar.

As a general rule the altar contributed to the dietary of the priests. But in verses 10 and 11 he reminds them of the notable

---

5. Canon Eden, *Theological Dictionary*, p. 19.
6. Bishop Lightfoot, *Philippians*, p. 181. See note on Heb. 13:10.

exception to that rule. The great annual sin offerings of the Day of Atonement, of which the blood was brought into the sanctuary, were "burned without the camp," and the priests had no right to eat thereof. Regarded in its highest aspect, we can have no part in the sacrifice of Calvary, even though we receive to the full the benefits and blessings accruing from it: *"Alone* He bore the Cross!" But the Cross testified, not only to God's judgment upon sin, but to man's estimate of the Sin bearer. It told not only of the wrath of God, but of the reproach which men heaped upon Christ. Is the Christian, then, to share the blessings, and yet refuse to share the reproach? Surely not: "Therefore [emphatic] let us go forth unto Him without the camp, bearing His reproach" (Heb. 13:13). This is the teaching of the passage.

Though expositors are generally agreed that it refers to the Day of Atonement, they differ as to whether the altar of sin offering has its antitype in the Cross or in Christ Himself. This betrays strange ignorance of the language in which Christian truth is revealed in the New Testament, namely, the typology of the Pentateuch. For there was no altar of sin offering. And upon the Day of Atonement the sin offering victim was not killed upon an altar at all. The law is explicit; it was killed *"beside* the altar." And neither altar nor priest is necessary to a sacrifice. For there was neither altar nor priest in Egypt when the great Paschal sacrifice of Israel's redemption was offered. And, moreover, the institution of sacrifice is as old as the Eden Fall.

Until we come to the heavenly visions of the book of Revelation, the New Testament knows nothing of an altar. The word is used eight times in the Gospels and six times in the Epistles; but only by way of narratival mention. Has the Christian then no altar? Assuredly he has; but its place is in the heavenly shrine of the Great High Priest. Altars and priests upon earth bear testimony, not to the Divine Presence, but to the apostasy of the professing church.[7]

---

7. The above passage is dealt with more fully in the author's work, *The Hebrews Epistle;* as are also the preceding texts from Hebrews.

*Anointing him with oil in the name of the Lord* (James 5:14).

The following is the Revised Version reading of the passage from which the above words are taken: "Is any among you sick? Let him call for the elders of the church; and let them pray over him, anointing him with oil in the name of the Lord: and the prayer of faith shall save him that is sick, and the Lord shall raise him up; and if he have committed sins, it shall be forgiven him. Confess therefore your sins one to another, and pray one for another, that ye may be healed (James 5:14-16)."

Save for one word that needs explanation for English readers, the New Testament contains nothing simpler and plainer than this, and yet nothing that is more misunderstood and perverted. Upon it is founded "the sacrament of extreme unction"; and, *misarabile dictu*! certain ultra-evangelicals use it as a scriptural basis for a practice akin to that of the Roman Catholic church.

In our English Testament "anoint" stands for two wholly different Greek words, the meaning of which is thus explained in Archbishop Trench's *Synonyms*: "*Aleiphein* is the common and mundane, *chriein* the sacred and heavenly word. Aleiphein is used indiscriminately of all actual anointings, whether with oil or ointment; while chriein, no doubt in its connection with *Christos*, is absolutely restricted to the anointing of the Son, by the Father, with the Holy Spirit, for the accomplishment of His great office, being wholly separated from all secular and common uses. Thus, see Luke 4:18; Acts 4:27, 10:38; 2 Corinthians 1:21; Hebrews 1:9; the only occasions on which *chriein* occurs."

Classical English has no special word for *aleiphein*, but to *massage* with oil expresses its meaning. And "it was as a salutary and approved medicament" that the patient was to be thus massaged prior to intercessory prayer on his behalf (Kitto's *Cyclopaedia*). Most expositors, however, represent this anointing as a sacramental rite to be performed by the elders in virtue of their office. And the inaccurate reading "anointing him with oil" (which mars both our versions) lends itself to this error. But as it is certain that among Orientals the elders would not themselves massage a *female* invalid, it must not be assumed that they did so in other cases. The Revised Version marginal reading "having anointed him" is grammatically correct; but perhaps "after he has been anointed" would better suit our English idiom. The added words, "in the name of the Lord," are commonly taken as proof that the anointing was a sacramental rite. But this indicates ignorance of the true character of the Christian life; for it is to "common and mundane" acts that the exhortation refers, "Whatsoever ye do in word or deed, do all in the name of the Lord Jesus" (Col. 3:17).

The passage, I repeat, is clear and simple. And its teaching may be summed up in two words, namely, the use of means, and believing prayer. Hezekiah's case illustrates this in a striking way. For though the prophet Isaiah was divinely bidden to bring him a definite promise of recovery, he enjoined the recognized remedy of the fig poultice. "For it is usual in the East, even to the present day, to employ a poultice of figs as a remedy for boils" (*Speaker's Commentary*, 2 Kings 20:7). The precedent is singularly apt. For the king was evidently dying of a malignant tumor; and in such cases "a lump of figs" would no more avail to work a cure, than would a basket of bread and fish suffice to feed thousands of hungry men. But "the use of means" is a divine principle thus inculcated for our guidance. And if, in these days of ours, Providence has brought within our reach better medicaments than oil or figs, it behoves us to use them "in the name of the Lord," with trustful and thankful hearts. Do we ignore God if we use our eyes when traversing a dangerous street crossing? Or if we put on a life preserver when a ship is in peril? "God has no pleasure in fools!"

There is "a gift of faith." And if any Christian can trust God to heal his sickness, or to set his broken limb, without the use of means, we should thank God not only for his cure but for his faith. But faith is a *personal* gift (Rom. 14:22); and a Christian, who allows others dependent upon him to suffer through his failure to provide them with remedies which the Providence of God has brought within his reach, is guilty of conduct as utterly unchristian as one who in other respects fails to "provide for his own house" (1 Tim. 5:8). As for those who seek to corrupt and coerce their fellow Christians by this false teaching, they merit stern reprobation on the part of all who fear God and love the truth. They bring Scripture into contempt, and often betray devout but ignorant Christians into a course of conduct that brings them within the meshes of the criminal law.

We have no definite ground for assuming that the elders of James 5:14 possessed miraculous powers of healing. Indeed, the words, "The prayer of faith shall save the sick," are against such a supposition. But there is no doubt that the disciples of the ministry were thus endowed, and it claims emphatic notice that, in their mission of healing, they habitually[8] made use of the oil massage (Mark 6:13). These things are "written for our learning." And if those who were supernaturally gifted to heal the sick were divinely led to make use of ordinary remedies, it is surely our part to follow their example, without hesitation and in the fullness of faith. And we shall recognize that the anointing enjoined by this Scripture—the use of a well-known and well-accredited remedy—has nothing in common with the superstitious practice of touching the body here and there with a finger dipped in oil, whether by a Romish priest or an Evangelical Christian.

> *I beseech you as strangers and pilgrims, abstain from fleshly lusts* (1 Peter 2:11).

Words are like counters. They have no intrinsic value, but bear whatever meaning people put upon them. According to the dictionary, for example, a pilgrim is "one who slowly and heavily treads his way; a traveler; especially one who travels to a distance from his own country to visit a holy place." And as "religion" enjoins upon people to become pilgrims, some sensitively devout folk will set out for Jerusalem or Mecca or Rome, while others will set themselves morbidly to practice asceticism. But the Bible nowhere enjoins upon the Christian to become a pilgrim. For while the aim which human religion sets before its devoted people is always to become something that they are not, the true effort of the Christian life is to realize and live up to what God's grace has made us.

But who and what is a pilgrim? The *parepidêmos* of the New Testament is one who is living away from his own country or people. How aptly this describes those who are born from above, and whose citizenship is in heaven! To take a sublunary exam-

---

8. This is indicated by the tense of the verb in the Greek.

ple, our relations and friends in India are pilgrims. Even though they spend a lifetime there, Britain is their home. This does not make them useless as residents of India, or careless in the discharge of their public and private duties there. And there may be nothing of the pilgrim about them in the dictionary sense. But they are pilgrims all the same.

It was not in order to become a pilgrim that Abraham left his palatial home and became a wanderer; but his faith vision being set on the heaven-built city of the divine promise, he confessed that he *was* a stranger and a pilgrim upon earth (Heb. 11:10, 13). So here, the First Epistle of Peter is addressed to "the elect who are pilgrims of the dispersion"; and it is to such that the appeal is addressed, "I beseech you as sojourners and pilgrims to abstain from fleshly lusts."

And here we have exhausted the passages in which the word occurs. For though it holds so large a place in the religion of Christendom, it is used but three times in the New Testament. Kindred teaching, however, abounds. That life on earth is but a pilgrimage is, indeed, in the very warp and woof of Christianity. The fact, moreover, that it is transient and brief is stamped indelibly upon the human heart. This, indeed, is one element in "the weight of that awful sadness, of which, to the mass of men, life is the synonym and the sum." But while for those who have no hope beyond the grave, the fleeting character of life on earth may well give cause for sadness and gloom, it ought only to deepen in the Christian's heart a sense of the true significance and value of our sojourn here, and of the eternal gladness and glory of the life to come.

*His own self bare our sins in His own body on the tree* (1 Peter 2:24).

"Most modern scholars are agreed to reject 'on the tree' in favor of the marginal 'to;' the proper meaning of the Greek preposition, when connected (as here) with the accusative, being what is expressed in colloquial English by 'on to the tree.' "

This sentence from Bishop Ellicott's *New Testament Commentary* is followed by a reference to the meaning that the Lord "offered up our sins in His own body on the altar of the cross."

That such a view should have the sanction of eminent names exemplifies the dictum of one of the great German theologians, that "the elucidation of the doctrine of the types is a problem for future theologians." In other words, theologians have neglected the study of the language in which Christian truth is revealed in the New Testament. The Hebrew Christians to whom the epistle was especially addressed would have stood aghast at such a pagan suggestion as that Christ was offering up sins to God; and upon an altar! The words of chapter 1:18, 19, would turn their thoughts at once to the Passover in Egypt; and no less instinctively would their minds revert to the scapegoat of the Day of Atonement as they read the words of 2:24.

"Bearing sins" is a figurative expression. But the figure is neither poetic nor forensic. It is explained by the ritual of the sin offering. In Leviticus 16:21, 22, we read, "Aaron shall lay both his hands upon the head of the live goat, and confess over him all the iniquities of the children of Israel, putting them upon the head of the goat . . . and the goat shall bear upon him all their iniquities into a land not inhabited"—the desert aptly symbolizing death. The ritual thus typified the amazing mystery of redemption—the imputation of our sins to Christ. The 22nd Psalm reveals His anguish when He reached that dread crisis of His mission. To read it as denoting His relations with His Father during all His earthly ministry indicates that in the religious sphere nothing is too profane or too foolish to be believed!

It was as God's representative that Aaron laid the people's sins upon the scapegoat. It was God Himself who laid our sins on Christ. And what the type foreshadowed, our passage tells us plainly, that this was *before* the Cross. The crucifixion was man's work altogether; witness the words this same apostle addressed to the Jews at Pentecost, "Him being delivered up by the determinate counsel and foreknowledge of God, ye have taken and by wicked hands have crucified and slain" (Acts 2:23). During all His ministry, no hand was ever laid on Him, save in loving service. But at times His immunity from threatened outrage was explained by the words, "His hour was not yet come." Now, that hour had struck; and the warning He had given the disciples was fulfilled: "The Son of Man shall be delivered into the hands of men" (Luke 9:4). Hence His words when His enemies approached Him in Gethsemane, "This is your hour and the power of darkness" (Luke 22:23).[9]

Judas delivered Him to the Jews, and the Jews delivered Him to the Roman power. But the words "delivered into the hands of *men*" can only mean that God delivered Him up in pursuance of His determinate purpose. And to this extent Scripture lifts the veil which shrouds the mysteries of Gethsemane, that then it was that the Lord Jesus passed under the load of the sins which He bare "in His own body to the tree."

*He went and preached unto the spirits in prison* (1 Peter 3:19).

"The literature of this passage is almost a library in itself" (Alford). And even the briefest review of that literature would exceed the limits of these notes. During a study of the passage extending over half a century I have sought for an exposition of it which would take account not only of the apostle's actual words and their context, but also of the scope and burden of the epistle in which it holds such a prominent place; and I know of at least one that satisfies these requirements.

First Peter was written to comfort and "establish" the saints during one of the terrible persecutions which devastated the early church. And the burden of it is that their sufferings were transient, and their triumph assured, the sufferings and glories of Christ being appealed to as the great exemplar. And here we may well ask, Even if the heresy of "a Protestant purgatory," as it has been aptly termed, were divine truth, could anything more egregiously inappropriate be introduced to crown the apostle's exhortation to steadfastness? For if even the heinous sinners of the antediluvian age were so especially favored, the

---

9. The prevailing misconception respecting this truth has been used to give plausibility to one of the grossest blasphemies of the Christianized infidels who, in these days, pose as Christian ministers. For if Christ's sufferings were purely physical, the profane might compare them with the sufferings endured by human martyrs and heroes. As one of the evil tribe has written, "Many a British soldier has died as brave a death as Jesus . . . An immense amount of pious nonsense has been spoken and written about our Lord's agony in Gethsemane . . . Your agony would be just as great as that of Jesus."—*The New Theology*, pp. 123, 124, 125.

Christians might surely assume that, if they turned from the path under pressure of such terrible persecution, they would certainly be granted mercy and "a second chance"; and thus the faithful and the unfaithful would reach the same goal at last.

Who then were they to whom the gospel was thus preached in the underworld? The answer is that there is nothing in our text about "preaching *the gospel*"! The word the apostle uses (*kerusso*) means "to proclaim as a herald," or "as a conqueror" (Grimm's *Lexicon*); and the context must decide the nature of the proclamation. When the word is used of preaching the gospel, this is always plainly indicated.

But then who were these "spirits"? Now, first, it is noteworthy that in Scripture, although human beings are said to have spirits, they are not usually called "spirits." "Souls" is the term used of them, even when disembodied (Rev. 6:9). But angels are generically designated "spirits." See, for example, Hebrews 1:7, 14. So again in Acts 8 "an angel of the Lord," in verse 26, is referred to in verse 29 as "the spirit." And, secondly, we must not isolate 1 Peter 3:19. It should be studied together with 2 Peter 2:4 and Jude 6, 7. And all must be read in connection with Genesis 6:1-7, to which these Scriptures so plainly refer.

Now Genesis 6 may be taken in either of two ways. The sceptic reads it with interest as a piece of ancient folklore, which was probably suggested by some tradition that a race of giants had once appeared on the earth. The Christian reads it with awe as explaining why a God of mercy and love "spared not the old world." The awful judgment of the Flood was not inflicted to punish the natural human sins of one generation of the inhabitants of earth—that is not God's way—but to exterminate a race that had become "corrupt" in the special sense here indicated; a corruption which, if left to work unchecked, might have tainted even the stock of which the promised "seed of the woman," the Redeemer of our race, was to be born.

Here then is the clue to the meaning of these references to "the angels that sinned" in antediluvian times. To suppose that human beings who gave themselves up to immoral practices would be called "the sons of God" is an extraordinary freak of exegesis. But that angels should be thus designated (as in Job

2:1 and 38:7) will not seem strange to any who have studied the biblical use of the word "son." Moreover the Lord Himself has decided this for us. In answer to the Sadducean quibble that the ordinance of marriage vetoed the doctrine of the resurrection, the Lord replied that the glorified of earth are "equal to the angels and are sons of God, being sons of the resurrection" (Luke 20:36, R.V.). Marriage pertains to an economy of natural bodies—the flesh and blood bodies of this world, whereas in that world we shall have spirit-bodies like the angels.

And this throws light upon the statement of Jude that these angels of Genesis 6 "kept not their first estate (that is, their primary condition; *dignity* is Alford's word) but left their own habitation" (their proper habitation, R.V. ). This last word seems to denote a descent from heaven. But it is most noteworthy that in the only other passage where *oikētērion* occurs, it denotes the spirit-body of the glorified saints (2 Cor. 5:2); and this is the second meaning of the word in Grimm's *Lexicon*. These renegade angels left their spirit-bodies, to come down to the level of flesh and blood. How this was possible is not revealed, but the fact is clearly indicated.

It may be objected that if there had been such an angelic revolt in heaven within Old Testament times, a more explicit mention of it would be found in Scripture. But this admits of a ready answer. The absence of any mention of the kind points to the conclusion that these angels of Genesis 6 were a section of those who shared in Satan's fall. If we are to yield to the folly of reasoning and guessing in such a matter, we would regard it as utterly improbable that holy angels of heaven could fall so low at a single swoop; but not so, that angels who had already fallen should sink to a still lower depth of evil. Their sin, moreover, may well have been instigated by Satan in furtherance of his age-long plot and effort to defeat the promise of "the woman's seed."

Although these angels are said to be "kept in chains under darkness," it is not said that the angels who fell with Satan were thus imprisoned; and we know that a host of them will yet take part in the mysterious war predicted in Revelation 12:7.

And now we can read this most difficult of all difficult texts in a new setting and with a new meaning. Its aim and purpose, I repeat, was to cheer and establish the suffering saints by unfolding the suffering and glory of Christ. And the "argument" of the teaching is that the height of His triumph was proportionate to the depth of His suffering. The prophecy of the 24th Psalm was fulfilled when, in open view of all the angelic hosts, He passed through the heavens (Heb. 4:14, R.V.). They had wondered at His sufferings, and now they were called to worship Him as Conqueror (Heb. 1: 6).

But, more than this, the apostle was inspired to tell that the Lord had proclaimed His triumph even to the apostate angels who had scorned His authority in antediluvian days. In translating the *kai* of this sentence by "also" our versions render it superfluous and meaningless, whereas it is intensely emphatic. "So complete was Christ's triumph that He led captivity captive (Eph. 4:8); so complete that, having spoiled principalities and powers, He made a show of them openly (Col. 2:15). So completely were angels and authorities and powers made subject unto Him, that His triumphal proclamation reached even to Tartarus—even to these imprisoned spirits."[10]

> *The like figure whereunto even baptism doth also now save us*  (1 Peter 3:21).

The meaning of this text is made clear by a more literal rendering of the words. The following is based on Dean Alford's *Commentary*: "Which [water, not baptism] the antitype [of the water of the Flood] now saves you also [as it saved Noah] even baptism."

The apostle's teaching is that, as the water which engulfed the world bore up the ark, Noah was saved from death by death, so also is the sinner who believes in Christ. For when he is united to Christ he becomes one with Him in death. It is the same truth as that of the sprinkled blood of the Passover in Egypt. This verse, therefore, is not a veiled reference to the pagan doctrine of baptism according to the Eleusinian mysteries,

---

10. *The Spirits in Prison*, by the late Rev. E. W. Bullinger, D.D., to whose exposition of the passage I acknowledge my indebtedness.

but plain teaching, which every Hebrew Christian would understand, that Noah's flood typified the death penalty upon sin, and Christian baptism symbolizes union with Christ in His death on Calvary.

> *For this cause was the gospel preached also to them that are dead, that they might be judged according to men in the flesh, but live according to God in the spirit* (1 Peter 4:6).

Any one who studies the literature of this verse with a free and open mind may well incline to the suspicion that its meaning is an unsolved problem—that it is, in fact, a lock of which the key has been lost; or, to explain my parable, that the apostle had in view some special circumstances or beliefs of which no record has come down to us.

We may clear the ground, however, by ruling out the mass of the expositions offered of it; as, for example, all such as depend upon putting a meaning upon the word "dead" different from that which it bears in the preceding verse (Alford). And we may assume that "the preaching of the gospel which is meant is before death, and not subsequent to it."[11]

We may also definitely assume that the apostle expected those whom he was addressing to understand his words; and further that they were designed to comfort and strengthen them in view of the calumnies and persecutions of evil men who resented their pure and upright manner of life. And yet some expositors ask us to believe that, to this end, he announced that Christ preached the gospel to those who perished in Noah's flood! And the suggestion is no less extraordinary, that they were to find comfort in the fact that those of their persecutors who were dead had heard the gospel after death, in order "that they might be judged," i.e. that their punishment might be the greater.

If we take "the dead" here indicated to be, not the persecutors, but their victims, certain graver difficulties of the passage will disappear. The following is Dean Alford's statement of a view which he does not himself accept: "For this reason was the

---

11. Bengel, *op. cit.*, vol. 2, p. 751.

gospel preached to those among you who have suffered death at the hands of persecutors that they might indeed be judged, condemned, by human persecution as regards the flesh, but might live with God as regards the spirit."

This will seem still clearer if, in construing the verse, we take account of the significance of the Greek particles *men* and *de* (which are ignored in both our versions); and further, if we give to the phrases *kata anthrōpous* and *kata Theon* the meaning assigned to the latter in, for example, Romans 8:27. The verse as thus read would clearly suggest all appeal from the judgment of men to that of God in respect of their martyred brethren. And it might be freely rendered thus:

"For unto this end also to the dead were good tidings preached, that although they might be condemned according to the will of men as to the flesh [i.e. their natural life], yet they might live according to the will of God as to the spirit" (i.e. their spiritual and eternal life).

### *If the righteous scarcely be saved* (1 Peter 4:18).

The difficulty which this text presents to so many is mainly due, first, to their not knowing that the verse is word for word a quotation from Proverbs 11:31, in the LXX version (the Greek Bible); and secondly, to the meaning commonly put upon our English word "scarcely." According to the dictionary, the primary meaning of that word is "with difficulty"; and this is precisely the meaning which Grimm's *Lexicon* gives for the Greek word *molis*.

As Dean Alford so well says, "The *molis* does not induce any doubt as to the issue, but only *wonder*. If we be justified by faith in Christ, our salvation, however difficult and apparently impossible, is as certain as Christ's own triumph."

The passage, when thus understood aright, has a much-needed message for these days of ours. The evangelical revival of a past century recovered for us the great truth of grace enthroned; but some of the present-day phases of evangelicalism tend to make us forget the almost unbelievable wonderfulness of that truth, and the infinite cost at which our redemption has been won. And so, on every side, even real Christians are being corrupted by the heresy that salvation for all men is assured, and that the main difference between the believer in Christ and the rejecter of Christ is that the one will reach heaven long before the other. The consequences of accepting or rejecting Christ are eternal; and in these days we cannot give too great prominence to the awfully solemn warning of our text, "If the righteous be saved with difficulty, where shall the ungodly and sinner appear?"

*No prophecy of Scripture is of any private interpretation* (2 Peter 1:20).

An important treatise on this verse enumerates no less than eight "various interpretations" of it. This extraordinary diversity of opinion is largely due to the ambiguity of the word rendered "interpretation." For *epilusis* occurs nowhere else, either in the New Testament or in the Greek version of the Old; and it is rarely found in other Greek writings. And the kindred verb occurs only twice in the New Testament (Mark 4:34 and Acts 19:39). The word *idios*, moreover, is what grammarians call an "emphatic possessive"; and in 77 of its 113 occurrences it is rendered "his own," but nowhere else is it translated "private."

To understand our verse aright, it must be studied in relation to the context. In verses 16-18 the apostle cites the vision of the Holy Mount as exemplifying "the power and [future] coming of our Lord Jesus Christ"; and he adds, "We have the word of prophecy made more sure, whereunto ye do well that ye take heed" (R.V.). This absolutely bars the meaning that verse 20 is meant to teach that we cannot understand any unfulfilled prophecy; and the emphatic "for" (*gar*) of verse 21 indicates that both verses are but a single clause, leading up to what is the gist and climax of the apostle's argument, namely, "that no prophecy ever came by the will of man, but men spake from God being moved by the Holy Ghost."

Now, suppose the passage had to be deciphered from a clay tablet broken just where the ambiguous word occurs, and that it read, "Knowing this first that no prophecy of Scripture is of . . . for no prophecy ever came by the will of man," would any one have the least doubt that the gap should be filled by some words denoting origin or source. And, this being so, surely the only question open is whether the words before us admit of such a construction.

Most noteworthy is it, therefore, that this is precisely the reading which the eminent writer above cited selects among the eight possible interpretations namely, "that no prophecy is the result of private or uninspired disclosure." "The subject of discourse [he says] is the prophetic oracles contained in the Old Testament, which, the apostle proceeds to show, were equally to be depended on as was the voice from the excellent glory; forasmuch as they did not originate with man, but with the spirit of God."

The propriety of this view is strikingly confirmed by the fact that it has the approval of eminent commentators, who themselves adopt a different interpretation of the verse. Bloomfield, for example, after stating it fully, claims that the view he himself accepts "seems entitled to preference"; thus implicitly acknowledging that it is legitimate and worthy of consideration. And Dean Alford, after citing it as Luther's, remarks, "This is much confirmed by *ginetai*, which with a genitive, as here, is not *estin*, but rather seems to denote *origin*." And he adds, "And this appears to be Bengel's view." Bengel's note on the verse is that prophecy is altogether "of divine unfolding or revelation."

To English readers the concluding sentence of the chapter is apt to suggest the very error which the passage is intended to veto. For the familiar phrase, "being moved" to do or say this or that, may seem to imply that "moved by the Holy Spirit" means merely that the prophets were led by divine influence to proclaim "the truth that was in them." But the Greek word here employed is, in one of its various meanings, the strongest that could be chosen to emphasize what the preceding sentence asserts, that "no prophecy ever came by the will of man." It is used, for example, in Acts 27:15 and 17 to describe the utter helplessness of a sailing ship in a fierce gale of wind—"a *rushing*, mighty wind," as the word is graphically rendered in Acts 2:2.

In fact, no plainer language could be framed to refute that heresy of German scepticism, which now leavens the teaching of most of our British theological colleges, that the prophecies were a natural product of the spiritual intelligence of the holy men who uttered them.

*Where is the promise of His coming?* (2 Peter 3:4).

This is misunderstood because theological labels have been put upon its prominent words. In biblical use *epangellia* and *parousia* are, as a rule, rightly translated "promise" and "coming." But the primary and common meaning of the one is an announcement or proclamation; and of the other, a "being present," whether with reference to persons or to things. A study of the chapter plainly shows that the apostle is not dealing here with either the hopes or the heresies of Christians, but with the scoffing of unbelievers, who mock at the divine warning that the world shall at last be given up to judgment fire. It is not the inquiring appeal of a believer about the coming of Christ, but the taunt of a scoffer about the coming of the Day of God. Indeed, it is not an inquiry at all, but an exclamation (like, for example, Gal. 4:15).

Professor Tyndall's words may possibly be true, that "for millions of years the earth has been the theater of life and death." All that we know is that in the beginning (whenever that was) God created it, and that He did not create it "a waste,"[12] even though it had become a waste before the epoch of the Adamic creation. Second Peter 3:5-6 points back to the cataclysm referred to in Genesis 1:2, by which "the world that then was, being overflowed with water, perished." So also the world of the Adamic economy will be destroyed by fire, in the final judgment of the Day of Jehovah. And because God is longsuffering, that awful day is long deferred; for it will involve the final perdition of the ungodly (v. 7), whereas the coming of the Lord Jesus Christ will lead to the restoration of the covenant people, and bring widespread blessing to the world (Rom. 11:15).

A brief notice of the closing verses of the epistle may be opportune. The reference to the apostle Paul's epistles as "Scriptures" implicitly recognizes that they were divinely inspired. And this is fitted to increase our surprise at the language of verse 16, which seems to disparage the manner in which truth is there unfolded. This surely should lead us to accept the alternative rendering of the words, as referring, not to the mode

---

12. See Isaiah 14:18 (R.V.), where the same word is used as in Genesis 1:2.

in which "these things" are treated by Paul, but to the nature of the things themselves. That they are "hard to be understood" is abundantly proved by the writings of the Fathers, and by the fact that they are generally misunderstood to the present hour.

That the burden of the chapter is not, as commonly supposed, the Lord's coming, but the dread *dies irae* at the end of all things, is further indicated by the words of the closing doxology, "To Him be the glory both now and to the day of eternity"—a phrase which occurs nowhere else in the New Testament, and which cannot refer to the Lord's coming which is our hope, nor yet to His coming as Son of Man to inaugurate the future economy of the "millennial" kingdom.

# 6

## *Misunderstood Texts in Revelation*

*The Lord God omnipotent reigneth* (Revelation 19:6).

The scepticism which sometimes troubles real Christians is often a revolt against "orthodox doctrines" rather than against divine truth. And any one who views the world with unclouded mental vision might well doubt the truth of Scripture, and very especially during the progress of hideous war, if Scripture really taught that "the Lord God omnipotent is reigning." For, as Dean Mansell has so truly said, "There are times when the heaven that is over our heads seems to be brass, and the earth that is under us to be iron, and we feel our hearts sink within us under the calm pressure of unyielding and unsympathizing law."

In view of the ghastly tragedy of these Armenian massacres, and of the daily horrors of hideous war, the infidel may well demand, "Where is thy God?" And the taunt is not to be met by pious platitudes. But the teaching of Scripture is explicit, that He who is now reigning is the Son of God, the Crucified of Calvary, and therefore the Divine Throne is now a throne of grace. It is not that the providential, nor yet the moral, government of the world is in abeyance, but that in this age there is no direct punitive action against human sin. For "the Lord knoweth how to reserve the unjust *unto the day of judgment* to be *punished* (2 Peter 2:9)", and this is the day of grace.

A silent heaven is "the mystery of God." But there is an appointed limit to the era of that mystery. The apocalyptic visions record the loud-voiced cry of the martyrs slain in the awful persecution of "the great tribulation": "How long, O Lord, holy and true, dost Thou not judge and avenge our blood?" (Rev. 6:10). But they record also the answer given by the "mighty angel," who swears by the Eternal Creator that there shall be delay no longer, and that the mystery of God shall be finished when the seventh angel begins to sound. And when we turn the page we read that when the seventh angel sounded there were great voices in heaven, saying, "The sovereignty of the world is become the sovereignty of our Lord and of His Christ (Rev. 11:15)." And then, we are told, the wonderful beings who sit upon thrones before God fell upon their faces and worshipped, giving thanks to the Lord God omnipotent, because He had taken to Him His great power and had begun to reign, and because the time was come when He would give reward to His saints and to all who fear His name, and would destroy them that destroy the earth. In the visions following we read of the judgments poured out upon the earth, and of the praises of heaven because of the judgments—praises which reach a climax in the glorious anthem, "Hallelujah, for the Lord God omnipotent reigneth" (Rev. 6:9, 10; 10:6, 7; 11:15-18; 19:6).

It is not good for the Christian, therefore, to give way to despondency or doubt because that consummation is delayed; for a silent heaven is eloquent in its testimony to divine long-suffering, and above the darkening clouds of the mystery of God is the glorious sunshine of the reign of grace.

"Hast begun to reign" may seem too free a rendering of 11:17. But the versions of both Rotherham and Weymouth[1] adopt the much freer rendering, "hast become King." And it is only by some phrase of this kind that the force of the Greek aorist can be expressed in English. The "hast reigned" of our Authorized Version might seem to imply that the reign was over. And the "didst reign" of the Revised Version is still more open to that objection. Alford notices this in his *Commentary* on

---

1. *Rotherham Emphasized Bible* (Kregel Publications), p. 259 and *Weymouth New Testament in Modern Speech,* (Kregel Publications), p. 710.

Revelation 19:6, where, giving up the attempt to translate the aorist accurately, he falls back upon the "reigneth" of the Authorized Version. Here again both Rotherham and Weymouth read "hath become King." But this is clearly misleading, for God has always been King. And the crisis which marks the change of dispensation is expressed by the words, "Thou hast taken to thee thy great power" (11:17).

To both learned and unlearned, therefore, I humbly offer the following rendering of the great anthem: "Hallelujah, for the Lord God omnipotent has begun to reign."

> *The marriage of the Lamb is come, and His wife hath made herself ready* (Revelation 19:7).

> *I will show thee the bride, the Lamb's wife . . . and He showed me that great city the holy Jerusalem, descending out of heaven from God* (Revelation 21:9, 10).

These Scriptures are misread when they are taken as referring to the same epoch. For between the fulfillment of the nineteenth chapter and of the twenty-first there lies the entire era of the future "kingdom" dispensation. And if we are to study the Book of Revelation intelligently, these dispensational distinctions must be kept in view. As explained in preceding notes, this present age will end with that coming of Christ which is revealed in the Epistles. And not until after that great crisis will the apocalyptic visions receive their fulfillment. The Abrahamic seed will then have been restored to their normal position as the covenant people of God; even though, as foretold by the Lord Himself in Matthew 24, they will still have to endure the terrible ordeal of "the great tribulation" of Old Testament prophecy. But a special recompense for their sufferings is assured to them. For just as the members of the church of this dispensation—not "the professing church," which is drifting to its doom, but the true church which the Lord is building—are elected to heavenly glory as "the Body of Christ," so also the faithful martyrs of that awful persecution are to have a distinctive reward by election to heavenly glory as "the Bride, the Lamb's wife." And they will attain that blessedness before the beginning of the "kingdom" age. But though the nineteenth chapter records "the marriage of the Lamb," it is not till we come to the twenty-first chapter that we read of the manifestation of the Bride. This earth was cleansed with water before its refurnishing as a home for man.[2] But before it can be united to heaven, and made meet for the display of the heavenly glory of the Bride it must needs be purified by fire. So it is not until the vision of the new heaven and the new earth that the Seer is summoned to behold the Bride. And what he sees is "the holy Jerusalem descending out of heaven from God."

One of the earliest pages of the Bible records how Abraham relinquished his princely life in the city which in that age claimed to be the metropolis of the world.[3] Another Scripture of long ages afterwards tells us that it was his faith-vision of a God-built city that led him to make that great surrender, and to choose the pilgrim path. But it is not until we come to the very last page of the very last book of the Sacred Canon—the "stock-taking" book of all the Bible— that we find the realization of his promise and his hope. What proof is here of the "hidden harmony," the absolute unity, of Holy Scripture! And what a testimony this unity and harmony afford to its divine authorship (Gen. 12:1-4; Heb. 11:8-10; Rev. 21:10-27).

For this is Abraham's City, the vision of which changed the whole current of his life. Upon its twelve gates are written the names of his natural descendants—"the names of the twelve tribes of the children of Israel." It is "the City which hath *the* foundations" (Heb. 11:10, R.V.); "twelve foundations, and in them the names of the twelve apostles of the Lamb." We shall not find here the names of the great apostle of the Gentiles and his companion apostles, who were God-given "for the building up of the Body of Christ" (Eph. 4:11, 12); but only of the Twelve who are "to sit upon twelve thrones, judging the twelve tribes of Israel" (Matt. 19:28), the apostles who were called to share that ministry of which the Lord declared, "I am not sent but unto the lost sheep of the house of Israel" (Matt. 15:24; cf. Luke 22:28-30).

But, it will be asked, "Is not the church the Bride of Christ?"

---

2. 2 Peter 3:5; Genesis 1:2.
3. Colonel Conder, *The Critics and the Law.*

That traditional belief is a legacy from an ignorant age which assumed that God *had* "cast away His people whom He foreknew." It has no warrant in Scripture. The very phrase, "Bride of Christ," is unscriptural. The holy Jerusalem is the "Bride, the *Lamb's* wife." But is not the Lamb merely another name for Christ? After the king's last visit to his Duchy, he intimated that his title of Duke of Lancaster was to be used in his future visits. But if a cabinet minister presented himself at the palace for an audience with "the Duke of Lancaster," it would be suspected that nerve-strain had affected his brain! In the human sphere, distinctions of this kind are understood and scrupulously observed; but our use of the names and titles of the Lord of Glory is characterized by utter indifference and ignorance. The king's Lancaster title may be used only in connection with his Duchy. And the fact that the Lord assumes His title of the Lamb in relation to His Bride, the heavenly city, is no warrant for using it in relation to "the church which is His body." Scripture never uses it in that connection. And the Epistles of the New Testament, which reveal the "mystery" truths of this Christian dispensation, will be searched in vain for a single mention of it (see note on Eph. 5:25, *ante*).